200
Decorative Title-Pages

Edited by Alexander Nesbitt

Associate Professor
Rhode Island School of Design

Dover Publications, Inc., New York

Published in the United Kingdom by Constable and Company Limited, 10 Orange Street, London W.C.2.

200 Decorative Title-Pages is a new work, first published by Dover Publications, Inc., in 1964.

Standard Book Number: 486-21264-5
Library of Congress Catalog Card Number: 64-16334

Manufactured in the United States of America
Dover Publications, Inc.
180 Varick Street
New York, N.Y. 10014

Foreword

"A foreword should contain nothing but the story of the book," said Gotthold Ephraim Lessing, the German author, in the foreword to his *Fables* of 1759. The story of the present book is simple: it grew out of another book, the author's *Decorative Alphabets and Initials** which, in turn, grew out of a collection of old books about initials and decorative letters. So well received was the earlier book, and so much interest did it arouse, that it struck me there might be a place for a book about decorative title-pages. There have been a good number of books about title-pages, but few of them were concerned with decorative titles exclusively or dealt with all periods of the printed book. It seemed logical, therefore, to attempt *200 Decorative Title-Pages*.

Some information about the development of the title-page is necessary for the inquiring user of this book. This is contained in the short essays that precede each of the three sections. The arrangement throughout is chronological. The first section deals entirely with early title-pages based on woodcut or metal-cut decoration. The second section is devoted largely to the engraved title up to the time of its disappearance in favor of the typographical title of the latter part of the eighteenth century. The third and final section of the book is concerned with the revival of the decorative title in the nineteenth century, and brings us up into our own century when once again the decorative title-page has been abandoned for the severe forms of functional typography.

What the future holds for the decorative title-page is anybody's guess. There are many indications, though, that the sterility and severity of the typography of the past forty years are

---

* Published by Dover Publications, Inc., in 1959.

undergoing a change.   It may be too soon to jump to conclusions, but a conjecture on the part of the author is that typography is tending once more to become decorative.

Each plate has been provided with a caption to show its place in the scheme of styles and usages, or to locate it in an area, assign it to a master, or give it a date.   A short Bibliography at the end of the book will help the aforementioned inquiring user to discover wider connections for himself.   The sources of the reproductions are also given there.

Most of the material in *200 Decorative Title-Pages* is hard to find in the original publications. Mr. Hayward Cirker collected a great deal of it; a small part is from my own collection.   The Hubert Goltzius title (Plate 71), that of the Cabinet Bible (137), *Paul et Virginie* (140), the William Pickering imprints (143, 144, 145, 148, 157, 158), and the two William Morris titles (168, 169) are from the personal collection of Mr. John R. Turner Ettlinger, curator of the Annmary Brown Memorial, Providence, who kindly lent them to me.   My task has been one of sorting and making selections; the goal was to produce a usable and rewarding book.

A. N.

Providence
August, 1963

I. The Period of the Woodcut Title

I. The Period of the Woodcut Title

In discussing the development of the title-page it must be stated immediately that titles first appeared in printed books. The manuscript book did not have this feature. Apparently early scholars felt that anyone worthy of the name would know very quickly what book he was in; extant literature was not too extensive and every genuine scholar knew most of it. Even the first printed books usually began simply with the Latin word "*incipit*," "here beginneth." With the rapid increase in the number of books, however, it became necessary to set aside a page to carry the title of the book and the miscellaneous information that would formerly have been placed in the colophon at the end. These first titles were not decorative; a few lines of type sufficed for this special purpose. The Erhard Ratdolt title of 1476 (Plate 1 shows the German edition of 1478) is generally considered the first ornamented page of this kind. It represents the beginning of a development that carried through to the middle of the next century, when all book ornament began to degenerate into a meaningless and disorderly overloading of the page with stock cuts and odd collections of much-used decorative material.

The Venetian title had the most profound influence on the use of decorative title-pages in western Europe. Accordingly, our first examples are a group of these early frames and borders. It is apparent that they derive directly from the Renaissance revival of classic ornament. As the influence moves into the Swiss and south-German areas a quite different effect is achieved by the *Formschneider*. These were the cutters—who were at times also the artists—that produced the actual printing blocks of wood or metal. One has only to compare the *Sachsenspiegel* title of Daniel Hopfer (13) with the title used by Gregorius (4) to see the different approach to ornament. In the Hopfer work there is much that is more related to Gothic ornament than to the Renaissance. The German-area artists, Hans Holbein the Younger (14,

16, 17, 27, 35), Hans Burgkmair (15, 20), Hans Baldung Grün (29), Urs Graf (12), and others, approached the book-title with a different feeling from that of the Italian-area artists, although they too used the elements of classic ornament. Just a simple visual investigation will reveal most of the difference. It is a matter of texture, movement, and the unique use of the classic forms.

By the time the Italian and German areas had passed the period of their finest book decoration the productions of the French area, especially Paris and Lyons, began to excel. The Renaissance influenced the sphere of the book later in France than anywhere else. It was Francis I who protected, nurtured, and expedited the young art of the book. The man whose name leads all others in the history of French book ornament is Geoffroy Tory (30, 31); he had worked and studied in Italy, and brought his powers to bear specifically on the art of the book. He was followed by men like Oronce Finé (36, 37, 40, 45), Bernard Salomon (53), and Jean Cousin the Younger (58), all of whom produced work of great quality and style.

A final burst of glory in the German area is to be found in the titles and ornaments of such diverse men as Hans Sebald Beham, Virgil Solis (56), Hans Brosamer, Jost Amman (57, 59, 63), and Tobias Stimmer (66). Their work spans the third quarter of the sixteenth century, lapping over about a decade on each end; it is a period of grandiose, overrich forms, full of almost unlimited line effects.

The last point of greatness in this era seems to have been Frankfurt am Main, which had become the center of the book trade in western Europe. One after another cities such as Augsburg and Nürnberg had ceased to produce first-class decorated books; by the end of the sixteenth century even the late blossoming of Frankfurt and Paris was past. This entire epoch of the art of the book had come to an end. There were, of course, isolated examples of continuing good production; but the art of the book had to wait until the eighteenth century for the next great surge of creative activity.

A few English titles have been added to show the production in this area; they are of definite interest although they did not at any time reach the excellence of the productions of other European areas.

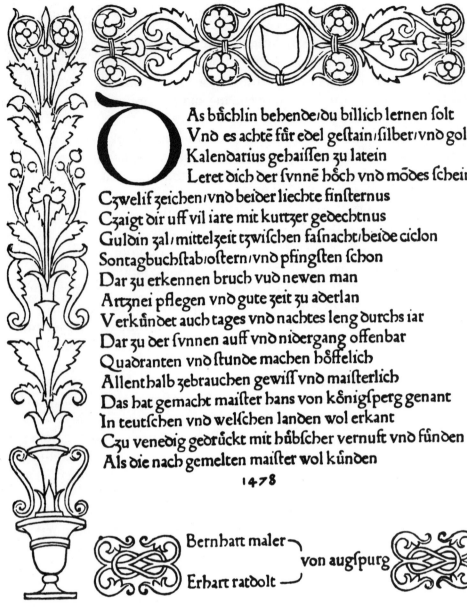

As bůchlin behende/du billich lernen solt
Vnd es achtē für edel gestain/silber/vnd golt
Kalendarius gehaissen zu latein
Leret dich der svnnē hóch vnd módes schein
Czwelif zeichen/vnd beider liechte finsternus
Czaigt dir uff vil iare mit kurtzer gedechtnus
Guldin zal/mittelzeit tzwischen fasnacht/beide ciclon
Sontagbuchstab/ostern/vnd pfingsten schon
Dar zu erkennen bruch vud newen man
Artznei pflegen vnd gute zeit zu aderlan
Verkündet auch tages vnd nachtes leng durchs iar
Dar zu der svnnen auff vnd nidergang offenbar
Quadranten vnd stunde machen hóffelich
Allenthalb zebrauchen gewiss vnd maisterlich
Das hat gemacht maister hans von kónigsperg genant
In teutschen vnd welschen landen wol erkant
Czu venedig gedruckt mit hůbscher vernuft vnd fůnden
Als die nach gemelten maister wol kůnden

1478

Bernhart maler
                              von augspurg
Erhart ratdolt

PLATE 1. Title-page of the Regiomontanus *Calendar*.   Erhard Ratdolt, 1478.

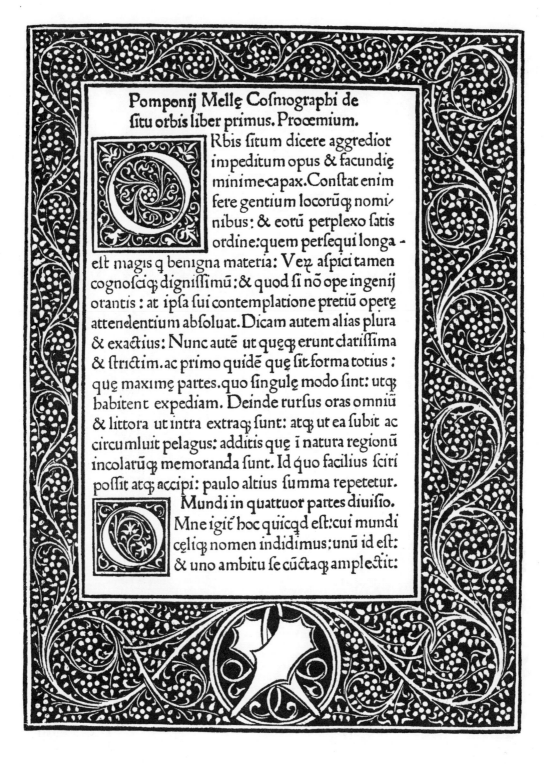

PLATE 2. Opening page of Pomponius Mela's *De situ orbis*. Erhard Ratdolt, 1478.

PLATE 3. Opening page of First Book of Livy. Printed in Venice, 1495.

PLATE 4. Often considered the finest piece of Renaissance book ornament. Gregorius, Venice, 1498.

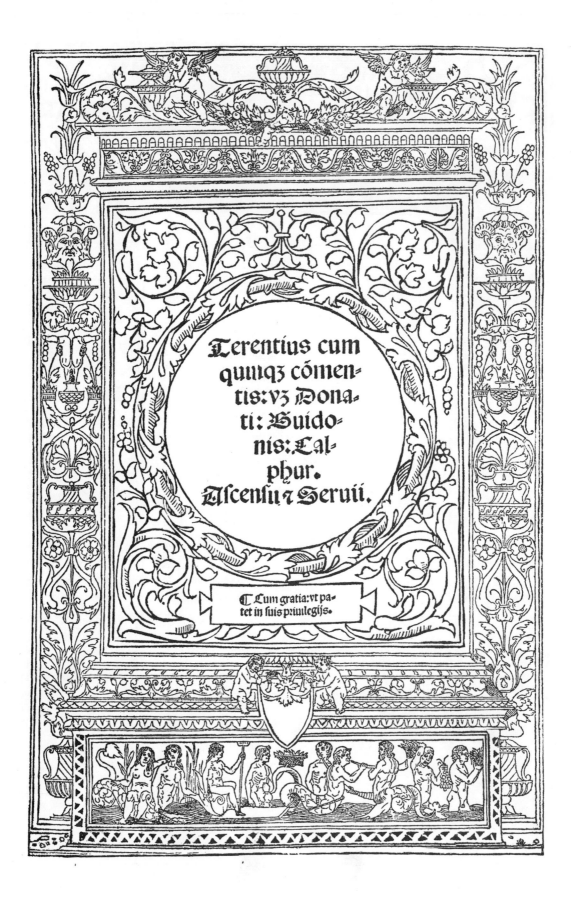

PLATE 5. Title to Terence, printed by Lazerus de Soardi. Venice, 1499.

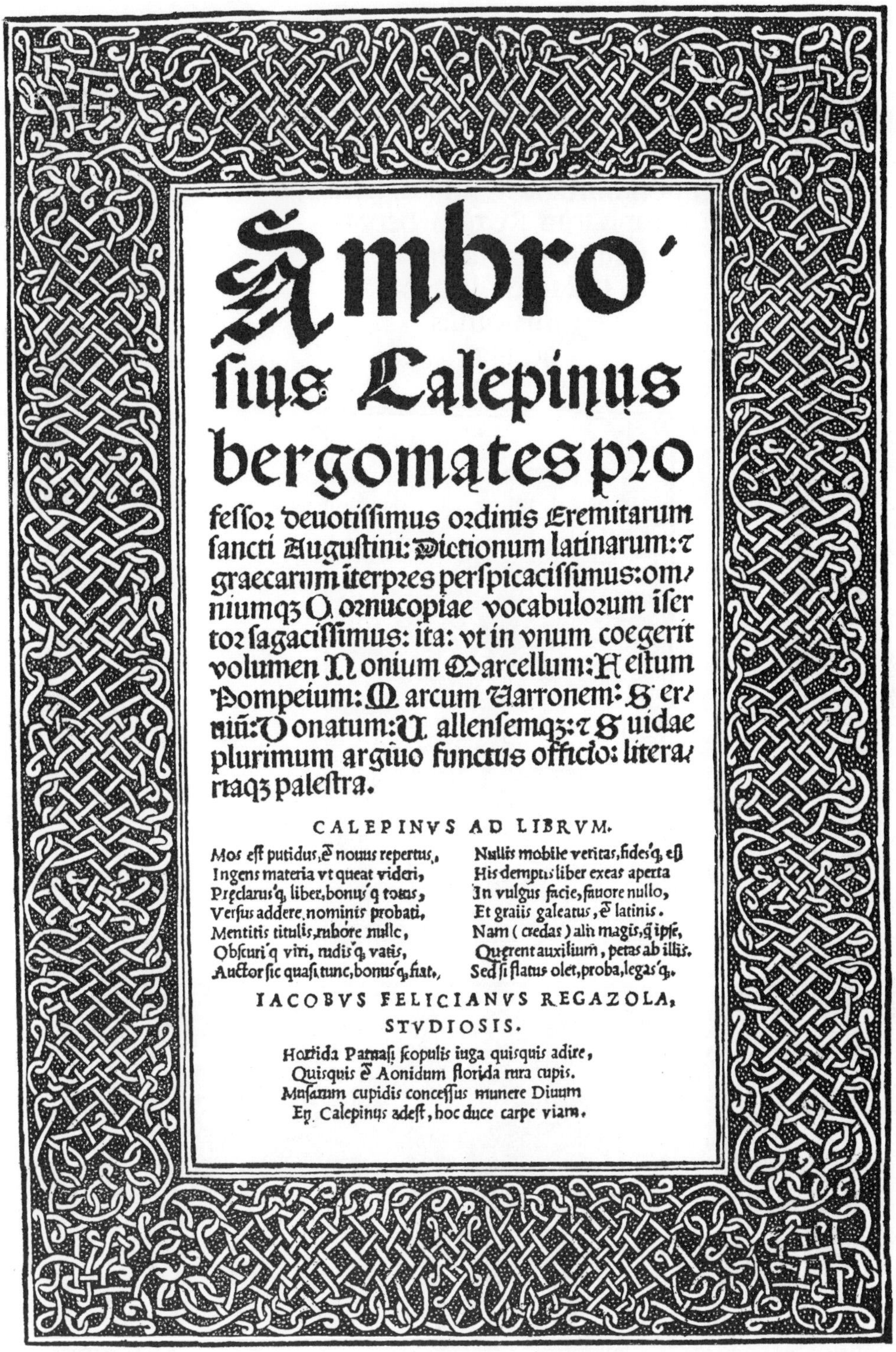

Ambro´sius Calepinus bergomates professor

deuotissimus ordinis Eremitarum sancti Augustini: Dictionum latinarum: z graecarum iterpres perspicacissimus: omniumqz Cornucopiae vocabulorum iser tor sagacissimus: ita: vt in vnum coegerit volumen Nonium Marcellum: Festum Pompeium: Marcum Varronem: Seruiu: Donatum: Vallensemqz: z Guidae plurimum arguo functus officio: litera riaqz palestra.

CALEPINVS AD LIBRVM.

Mos est putidus, & nouus repertus,
Ingens materia vt queat videri,
Preclarus'q, liber, bonus'q totus,
Versus addere nominis probati,
Mentitis titulis, rubore nulle,
Obscuri'q viri, rudis'q, vatis,
Auctor sic quasi tunc, bonus'q, fiat,

Nullis mobile veritas, fides'q, est
His demptis liber exeas aperta
In vulguis facie, fauore nullo,
Et graiis galeatus, & latinis.
Nam (credas) alii magis, q ipse,
Querent auxilium, petas ab illis.
Sed si flatus olet, proba, legas'q,

IACOBVS FELICIANVS REGAZOLA,

STVDIOSIS.

Horrida Parnasi scopulis iuga quisquis adire,
Quisquis & Aonidum florida rura cupis.
Musarum cupidis concessus munere Diuum
En, Calepinus adest, hoc duce carpe viam.

PLATE 6. A border in the Moorish style.   Alessandro Paganini, 1500.

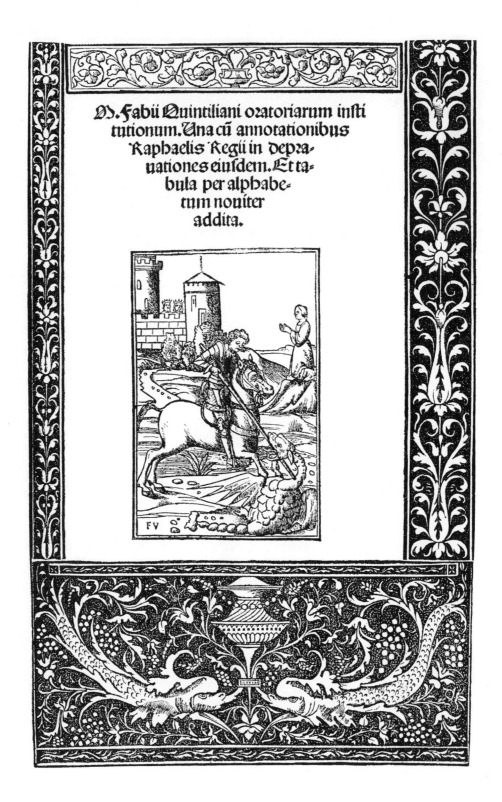

PLATE 7. Title made of pieces.   Gregorius de Rusconibus, Venice, 1506.

PLATE 8. A title used by Julian Notary. England, 1507.

AVLI GELII NOCTIVM ATTICARVM COMMENTARII.   LIBER PRIMVS.

PLVTARCHVS IN LIBROQ uem ὁπόση ψυχῶν καὶ σωμάτων ἀνθρώποις περὶ διαφυίαν καὶ ἀρετὴν διάφορα: idest quantum inter homines animi corporisque ingenio atque uirtutibus intersit: conscripsit: scite subtiliterq; rociriatum Pythagora philosophum dicit: in reperienda: moduladaq; status longitudinis eius praestatia. Nam quum fere constaret curriculum stadii: quod est pisis apud Iouem olympium: Herculem pedibus suis metatum: idq; fecisse longum pedes ducetos: caetera quoq; stadia in terris graeciae ab aliis postea instituta: pedum quidem esse numero ducentorum: sed tamen esse aliquantulum breuiora: facile intellexit modum: spatiumq; plantae Herculis ratione proportionis habita: tanto fuisse q alioru procerius: quanto olympicum stadium longius esset: q caetera. Comprehensa autem mesura herculani pedis fm naturalem membroru omnium inter se copetentiam modificatus est. Atq; ita id collegit: quod erat consequens: tanto fuisse Herculem corpore excelsiorem: q alios: quanto olympicum stadium caeteris pari numero factis anteiret.

¶ Ab Herode attico consulari uiro tempestiue deprompta in quendam iactatum & gloriosum adolescentem: specie tantum philosophiae sectatorem uerba Epicteti stoici: quibus festiuiter a uero stoico seiunxit uulgus loquacium nebulonum: qui se stoicos nuncuparent.   Caput.ii.

Herodes Atticus uir & graeca facundia: & consulari honore praeditus: accersebat saepe nos: quum apud magistros athenis essemus: in uillas eius urbi proximas: me & clarissimum uiru Ser uilianum: coplurisq; alios nostrates: qui Roma in Graeciam: ad capiendum ingenii cultum concesserant. Atq; ibi tunc quum essemus apud eum in uilla: cui nomen est cephysia: & aestu anni: & sidere autumni flagrantissimo propulsabamus caloris incomoda lucoru umbra ingentiu longis ambulacris: & mollibus aedium posticum refrigerantibus lauacris nitidis: & abundis: & collucentibus: totiusq; uillae uenustate aquis undiq;

PLATE 9. Another Venetian opening page.   Giovanni Tacuino da Tridino, 1509.

℄ Secūda pars operis dñicæ paſſionis & reſurrectio
nis dié ídagat,& iudæoʒ ſup hoc argumēta confutat.

Tſi multa ſunt argumenta,
quibus iudæi magnam no
bis calumniā ſolent aſtrue
re,& fidem ſperatæ a nobis
reſurrectionis ſtulta garru
litate deridere,in hac tamē
lucubratiuncula·noſtra ea
duntaxat confutare aggre
diemur,quæ dominicæ paſ
ſionis & reſurrectionis materiam concernunt.Solet
nanqʒ obſtinatum illud, & ſeruile iudæorum pecus
in Chriſti ſaluatoris blaſphemiam exire propenſius
& in chriſtianorum calumniam inſultare audentius
& confidentius, quia legis noſtræ munimenta non
pauca ex auita ipſorum religione mutuati ſumus
ea præcipue,quæ agni paſchalis typo,domini paſſio
nem ſignificabant:quo fit ut perperam interpretan
tes legem,& diuini ſacra menti myſterium contami
nantes,multas indies calumnias nobis inferre nō de
ſiſtant,nunquam cauillandi finem facientes:adeo ǫ
cōtinuis ſubſānationibus nos laceſſentes,& ſingulas
obſeruationes noſtras deteſtātes perpetuis ipſoʒ cō
tumeliis,atqʒ conuitiis ſimus obnoxii:non ſolum in
paſchæ celebratione obſeruationé noſtram ludibrio
maximoqʒ opprobrio ducentes(de quo ſuperiori lu
cubratiuncula noſtra ſcripſimus)uerū etiam í dñicæ
paſſionis myſterio ruditatis,& íſcitiæ nos íſimulātes

A. ii

PLATE 10. Opening page, using pieces.   Ottaviano dei Petrucci,
Fossombrone, 1513.

PLATE 11. Another pieced title.   Johann Otmar, Augsburg, 1515.

AMPLISSIMO PATRI D. THOMAE RVTHALLO EPI
SCOPO DVNELMENSI SERENISSIMI BRITAN
NIAE REGIS SECRETARIO MAGNO
ERASMVS ROTERODAMVS S.D.

MIRE VIDETVR eueniſſe, Præſul ornatiſſime, ut utriɋ d uerſo ɋ
dem genere, ſed tamen haud ita diſſimilem militiam eodem tḗpo
re militauerimus. Etenim dum tu primū regis uere inuictiſſimi fe
licibus auſpicijs Gallos in fugam agis, deinde a caſtris in caſtra re
uerſus, Scotorum regem, maximis & inſtructiſſimis copijs, in ditiõis tuæ fines
irrumpentem repellis, fundis, conſcindis, ego duos omnium optimos, ſed om
nium deprauatiſſimos autores, Diuum Hieronymū, & Senecam, a mendis, te
terrimis uidelicet litterarum hoſtibus, quibus hactenus nõ cõtaminati fuerãt,
ſed prorſus extincti, ſummo ſtudio uindicaui. Et mihi cū geminis hoſtibus fuit
res, Nec uſɋ arbitror in ueſtris caſtris plus fuiſſe difficultatis, aut ſudoris, ɋ mi
hi fuerit in hoc negocio. Quanɋ hoc etiam uinco nomine, quod ūnus ipe dux
pariter ac miles, cum tot hoſtium milibus conſerui manum, Iam nec ſtrages in
hoc conflictu minor, ɋ in ueſtris prælijs. Nam aduerſus Gallos, quo minus cru
enta fuerit pugna, ciuilitas hoſtium (nam quo potius appellḗ nomine˂) in cau/
ſa fuit, qui ſic ad primum ſtatim congreſſum, ceſſere melioribus, ut appareret
in hoc ipſum ueniſſe, quo uobis prædam adducerent. Cæterum e Scotis ingḗs
quidem contigit uictoria, nimirum ipſo rege cum innumeris optimatibus cæ
ſo, & eo rege, qui gladiatorio (quod aiunt) animo, ſummam perniciem uniuerſæ
Britanniæ moliretur. Verum ea cõtigit multo ueſtratium empta ſanguine. At
ego unico conflictu, ſupra quatuor hoſtium, imo portentorum, milia, iugulaui,
cõfodi, deleui. Tot enim, opinor, mḗdas, uel ex uno Seneca ſuſtuli. Adde quod
Scotus miles uix primos Britannicæ ditionis fines fuerat ingreſſus, & unicam
duntaxat occuparat arcem, unde mox depulſus eſt. At totum Hieronymū, to
tumɋ Senecam, multis iam ſæculis infinitus mendarum numerus occuparat,
ut nihil uſɋ eſſet reliquum, quod non ab hoſtibus teneretur. Atɋ hac quidḗ in
re mihi pro gladio calamus fuit, pro Marte Muſæ, pro copijs ingenium. Nec ul
lum alioqui auxilium, in tantis rerum difficultatibus, præter duos uetuſtos codi
ces, quorum alterum exhibuit e ſua bibliotheca, ſummus ille meorum ſtudiorū
Mœcenas, & incõparabile noſtri ſæculi decus, Gulielmus Archiepiſcopus Can
tuarienſis, alterum, regium apud Cantabrigienſeis collegium ſuppetias miſit.
Sed utrunɋ primum mutilum, deinde uulgatis etiam exemplaribus mendoſi
orem, ut minus fidendum fuerit auxiliaribus copijs, ɋ ipſis hoſtibus. Illud ta
men profuit, quod nõ conſentiebant errata, id, quod accidere neceſſe eſt in his
libris, qui ex eodem exemplari formulis excudūtur. Proinde quemadmodum
aliquoties fit, ut peritus & attentus iudex, e multorum teſtium oratione, quorū
nemo tamen uerum dicat, rem colligat, ita nos e diuerſis mendis ueram conie.

a 2

IOANNES
FROBENI
VS SVIS
TYPIS
EXCV
DE
BAT

PLATE 12. An opening page used by Johann Froben. Basel, 1515. An Urs
Graf design.

Saffenspegel
mit velen nyen Addi-
cien fan dem Le-
enrechte vnde
Richtftige.

Ad lectorem Saphicum
cum Gliconico,

Saxonum dicor fpeculum, legenti
Leges, iuraꝗ tribuo;
Saxonum lingua loquor, ipfe Saxo
Per me iura leget fua.

PLATE 13. A famous woodcut title by Daniel Hopfer.   Used by Silvan Otmar,
Augsburg, 1516.

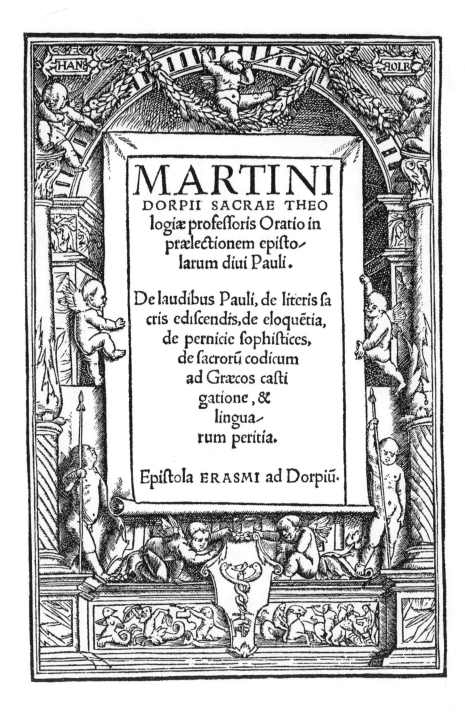

MARTINI
DORPII SACRAE THEO
logiæ professoris Oratio in
prælectionem episto-
larum diui Pauli.

De laudibus Pauli, de literis sa
cris ediscendis, de eloquétia,
de pernicie sophistices,
de sacrorũ codicum
ad Græcos casti
gatione, &
lingua-
rum peritia.

Epistola ERASMI ad Dorpiũ.

PLATE 14. A Hans Holbein the Younger design. Used by Johann Froben, Basel, 1516.

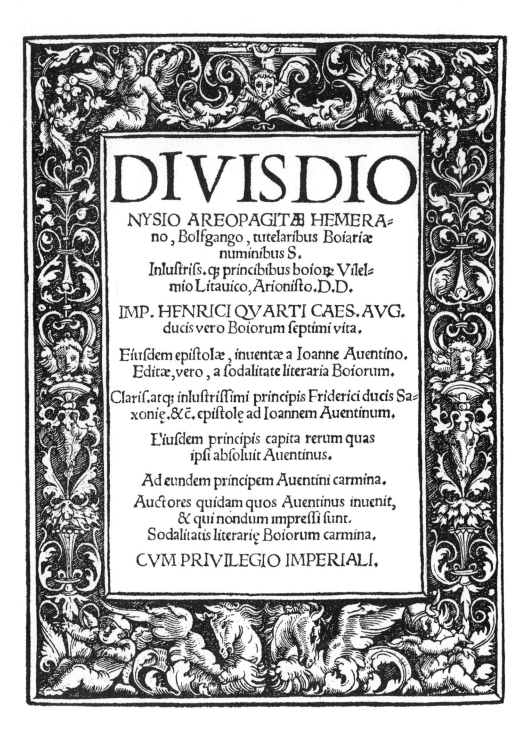

PLATE 15. A Hans Burgkmair design. Used by Grimm and Wirsung, Augsburg, 1518.

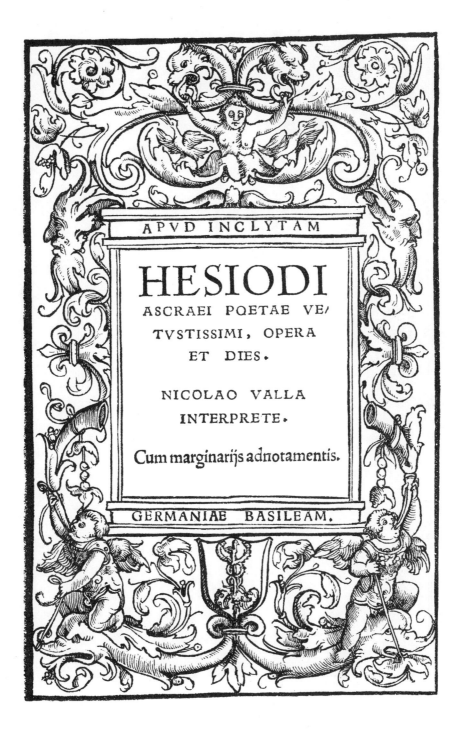

APVD INCLYTAM

HESIODI

ASCRAEI POETAE VE/
TVSTISSIMI, OPERA
ET DIES.

NICOLAO VALLA
INTERPRETE.

Cum marginarijs adnotamentis.

GERMANIAE BASILEAM.

PLATE 16. Another Hans Holbein the Younger title. Johann Froben, Basel, 1518.

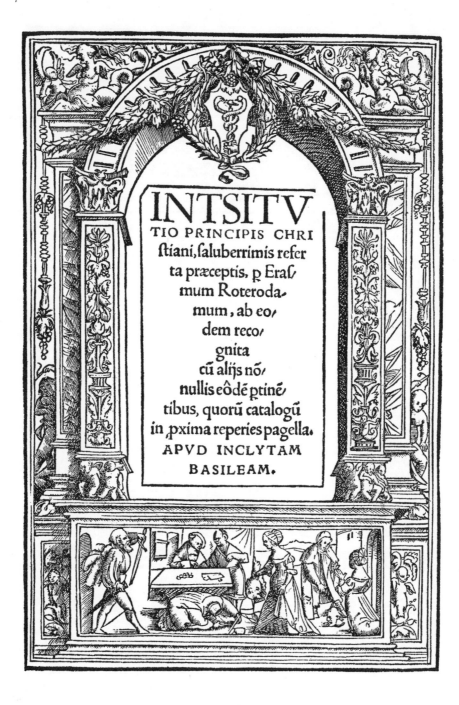

INTSITV
TIO PRINCIPIS CHRI
ſtiani, ſaluberrimis refer
ta præceptis, p Eraſ
mum Roteroda,
mum, ab eo,
dem reco,
gnita
cũ alijs nõ,
nullis eôdẽ ptinẽ,
tibus, quorũ catalogũ
in ‚pxima reperies pagella.
APVD INCLYTAM
BASILEAM.

PLATE 17. Hans Holbein the Younger title.   Another of the Froben series,
    Basel, 1518.

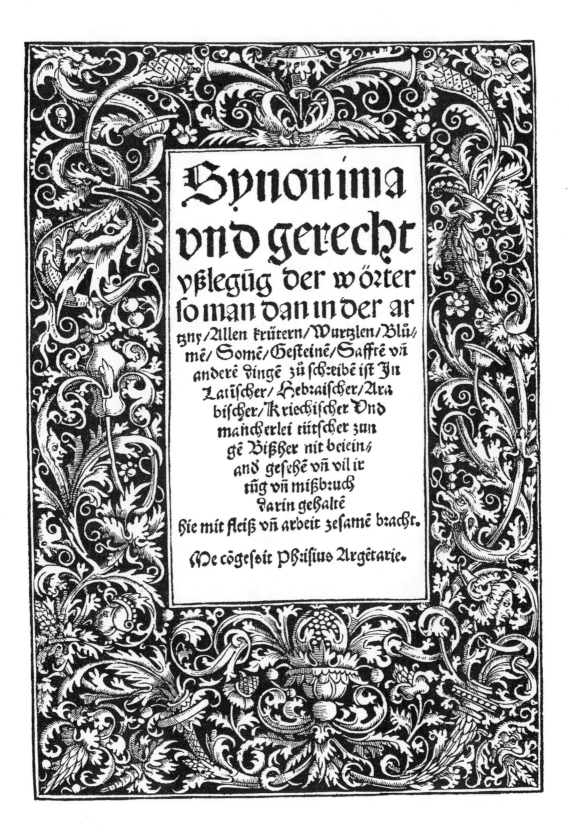

PLATE 18. A fine title, used by Johann Grüninger, Strassburg, 1519.

PLATE 19. The printers Sigmund Grimm and Marx Wirsung used this title,
Augsburg, 1519.

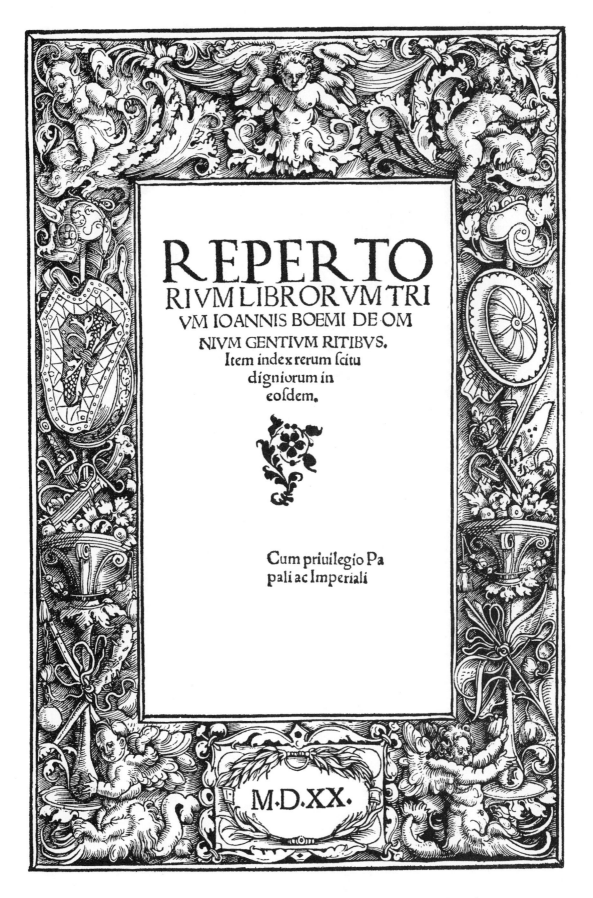

REPER TO
RIVM LIBRORVM TRI
VM IOANNIS BOEMI DE OM
NIVM GENTIVM RITIBVS.
Item index rerum scitu
digniorum in
eosdem.

Cum priuilegio Pa
pali ac Imperiali

M·D·XX.

PLATE 20. A Hans Burgkmair design for Grimm and Wirsung, Augsburg, 1520.

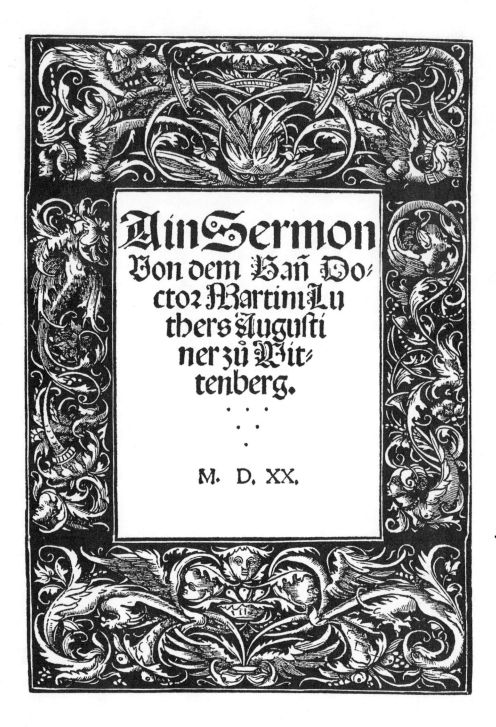

PLATE 21. Another Hopfer title, apparently pieced.   Silvan Otmar,
    Augsburg, 1520.

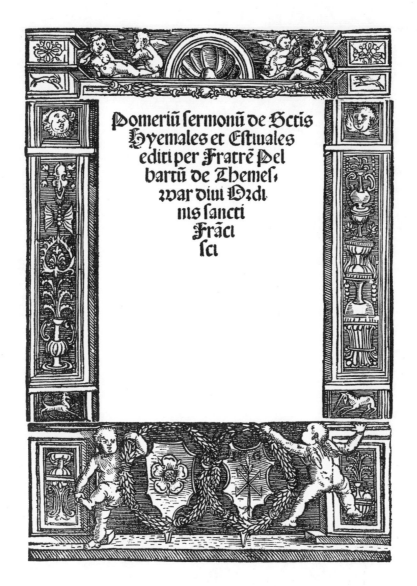

PLATE 22. Title made of pieces. Used by Wolf Köpfel, Strassburg, 1520.

HIERO
NYMI ECLOGA DE
LOCIS HEBRAICIS.

VVITTEMBERGAE.

PLATE 23. A Lucas Cranach design. Used by the Luther printer, Johann
Grunenberg, 1522.

PLATE 24. Moorish influence on Albecht Dürer. Used by Friedrich Peypus, Nürnberg, 1522.

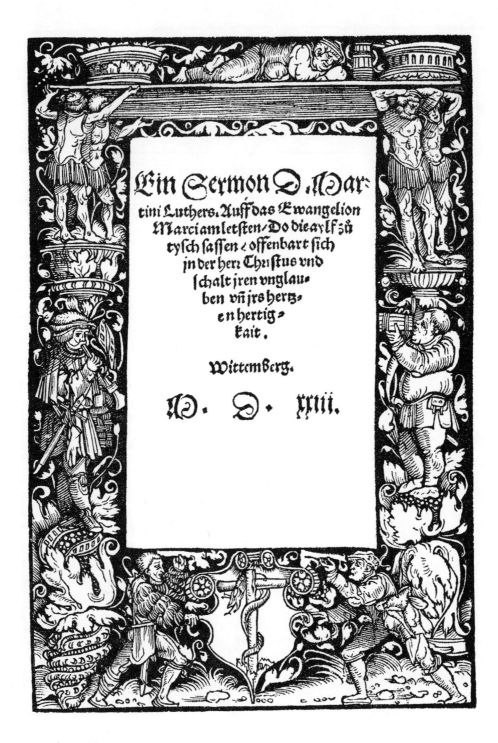

PLATE 25. Lucas Cranach title. Used by Johann Grunenberg (Georg Rhau), 1523.

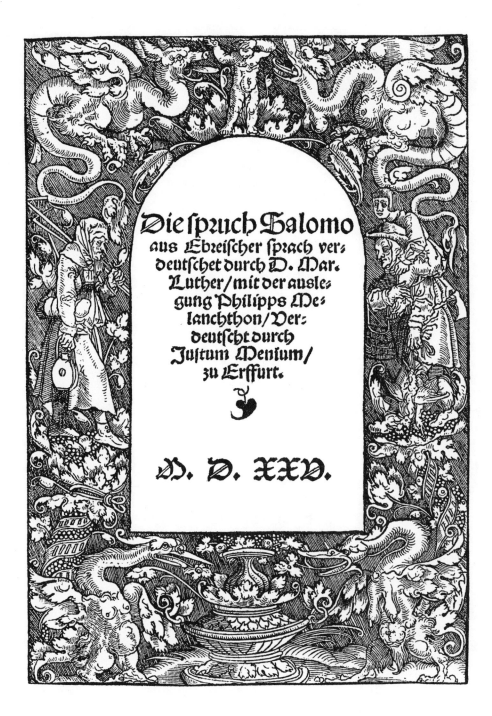

PLATE 26. A title in the style of the Saxon school.   Used in Erfurt, 1525.

PLATE 27. Hans Holbein the Younger's characteristic style. Used by Adam Petri in Basel.

PLATE 28. Title to Luther's tract against the rebellious peasants.   Wittenberg.

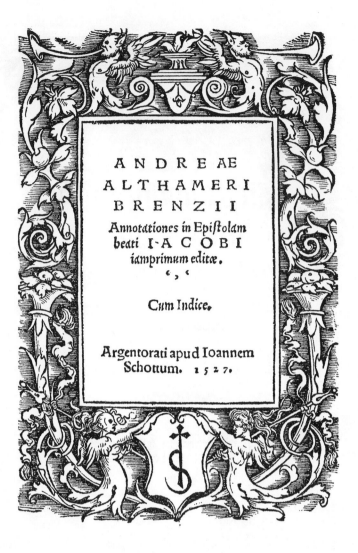

ANDREAE
ALTHAMERI
BRENZII
*Annotationes in Epiſtolam
beati* I·ACOBI
iamprimum editæ.
‘,‘

Cum Indice.

Argentorati apud Ioannem
Schottum. 1527.

PLATE 29. A title by Hans Baldung Grün. Used by Johann Schott, Strassburg.

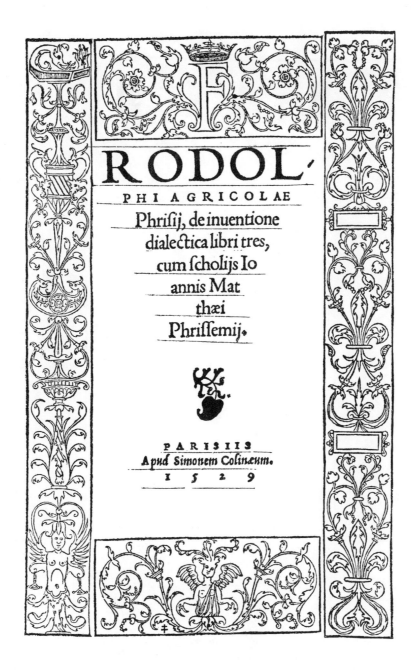

RODOL'
PHI AGRICOLAE
Phriſij, de inuentione
dialectica libri tres,
cum ſcholijs Io
annis Mat
thæi
Phriſſemij.

PARISIIS
Apud Simonem Colinæum.
1529

PLATE 30. A pieced title by Geoffroy Tory.   Used by Simon de Colines, Paris.

PLATE 31. Another Tory title. Used by Gilles Gourmont.

CRegistrum
omniū breuium
tam originaliū
ꝗ iudicia-
lium.

✠

LONDINI.
☞ Apud Guilielmum Rastell.

1531

☞CVM PRIVILEGIO.

PLATE 32. A title used by William Rastell, London, 1531.

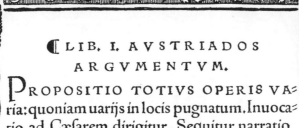

❡LIB. I. AVSTRIADOS
ARGVMENTVM.

Propositio totivs operis va=
ria: quoniam uarijs in locis pugnatum. Inuoca=
tio ad Cæsarem dirigitur. Sequitur narratio,
sed concise: quoniam alibi diffusius rei initium
narratur. Bellona tanquam Germanorum in re
militari gloriæ inuida, pugnam ab inferis De=
am, quam & Eumenides sequebantur, euocat:
a quibus Germanorum animi ad Martem ac=
cenduntur. Sequitur Roberti prius secum, de=
mum cum patre Philippo, de suscipiendo bel=
lo consultatio: cui pater persuadet, noscendam
esse Deorum uoluntatem, aramq3 Vlyssis ad
oceanum (unde responsa petebantur) adeun=
dam consulit: quod etiam Pallas in somnis Ro=
berto peragēdum imperat. Et per occasionem,
caussæ recensēt indignationis Deæ, qua Au=
striadas prosequebatur, quam in toto opere ho
stem Cæsaris facit, in fine redijsse in concordi=
am scribit. Itur ergo ad aram: ubi Robertus cū
sacerdote loquitur, a quo loci & origo narra=
tur, & umbrę ab inferis euocantur: quarum no
mina Georgius dux Roberto exponit:inibicȝ
multa de origine Magiæ. Interim sacerdos fun=
ctus sacro, bellum ingens, cædescȝ futuras ca=
nit. In fine umbrarum fuga describitur. Et Ro=
bertus non bene percępto oraculo, dulces ter=
ras, patriamcȝ reuisit.

PLATE 33. An opening page printed by Johann Schott, Strassburg, 1531.

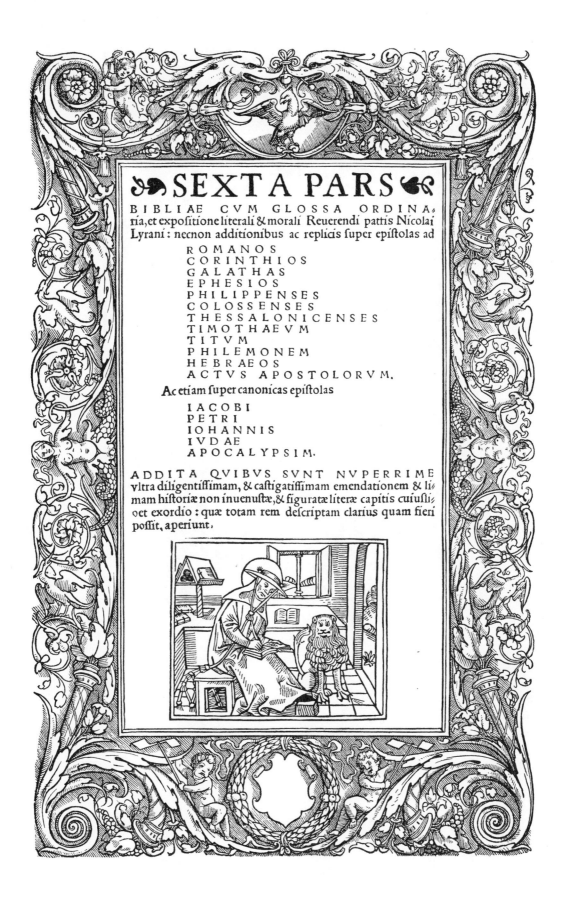

PLATE 34. A title used in the French area. Typical of the 1530's.

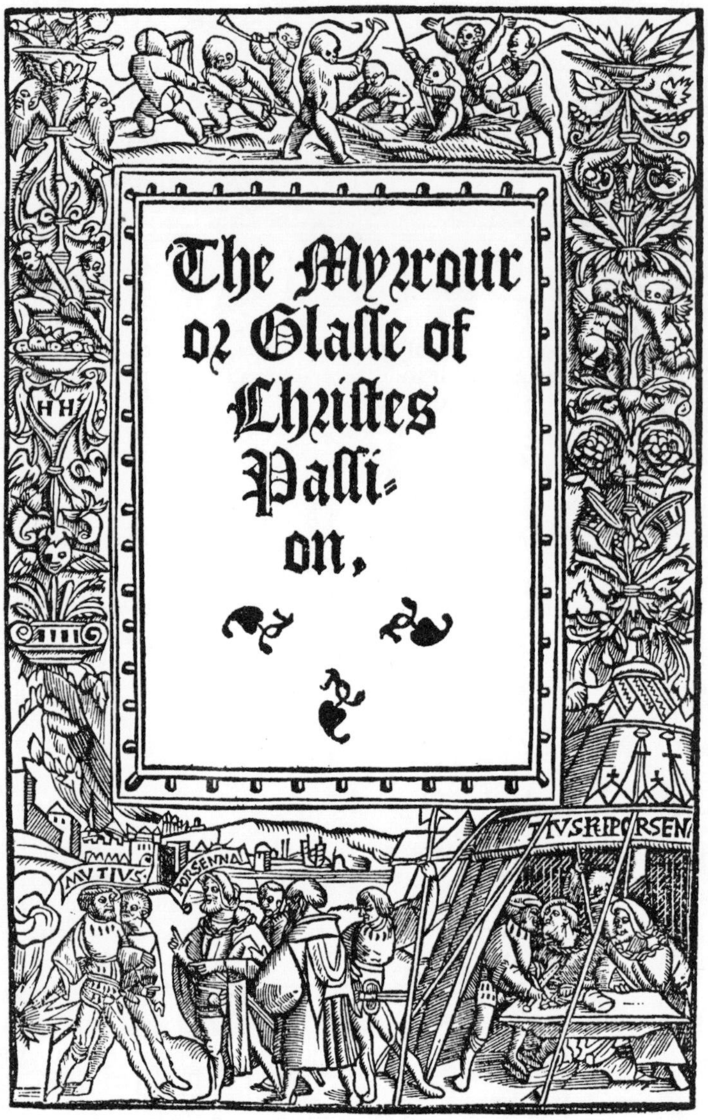

PLATE 35. English copy of a Hans Holbein the Younger title. Used in London, 1534.

ORONTII
FINEI DELPHINATIS, RE-
GII MATHEMATICARVM
PROFESSORIS:

QVADRANS
ASTROLABICVS, OMNI-
bus Europæ regionibus inferuiés:
Ex recenti & emédata ipfius Au-
thoris recognitione in amplioré,
ac longè fideliorem redactus de=
fcriptionem.

PARISIIS.
Apud Simonem Colinæum
1 5 3 4.

PLATE 36. An Oronce Finé title with criblé background. Used by Simon de
Colines, 1534.

Orontij Finei Del
PHINATIS, REGII
Mathematicarum
profeſſoris,

IN SEX PRIORES LIBROS
geometricorum elementorum
Euclidis Megarenſis De=
monſtrationes.

Quibus ipſius Euclidis textus græcus, ſuis locis inſertus eſt: vna cum interpretatione
latina Bartholamæi Zamberti Ve-
neti, ad fidem geometricã per
eundem Orontium
recognita.

CVM PRIVILEGIO
Regis ad decennium,

PARISIIS.
Apud Simonem Colinæum.
1 5 3 6.

Vireſcit vulnere virtus.

PLATE 37. Another Finé title.   Simon de Colines, Paris, 1536.

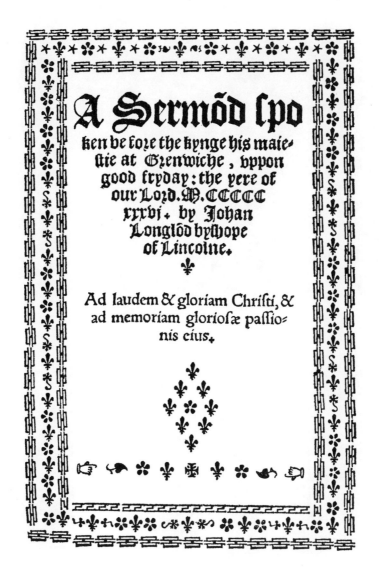

PLATE 38. Cast pieces as ornaments. London, 1536.

De Natura ſtir-
PIVM LIBRI TRES,
Ioanne Ruellio authore.

Cum priuilegio
R EGIS.

PARISIIS.
Ex officina Simonis Colinæi.
1 5 3 6.

PLATE 39. The title to a famous book.   Simon de Colines, 1536.

DE STVDIO

LITERARVM rectè & cómodè insti-
tuédo, ad inuictissimũ & potétissimũ Princi-
pé FRANCISCVM, Regé Fráciæ: Gu-
lielmo Budæo Parisiensi, Cósiliario regio, Li-
bellorũq; supplicũ in Regia Magistro, auctore.

Excudebat Michael Vascosanus, in ædibus
Ascésianis, via ad D. Iacobũ, sub signo Fótis.
PARISIIS,   M. D. XXXVI.

PLATE 40. A Finé title used by Michel Vascosan, Paris, 1536.

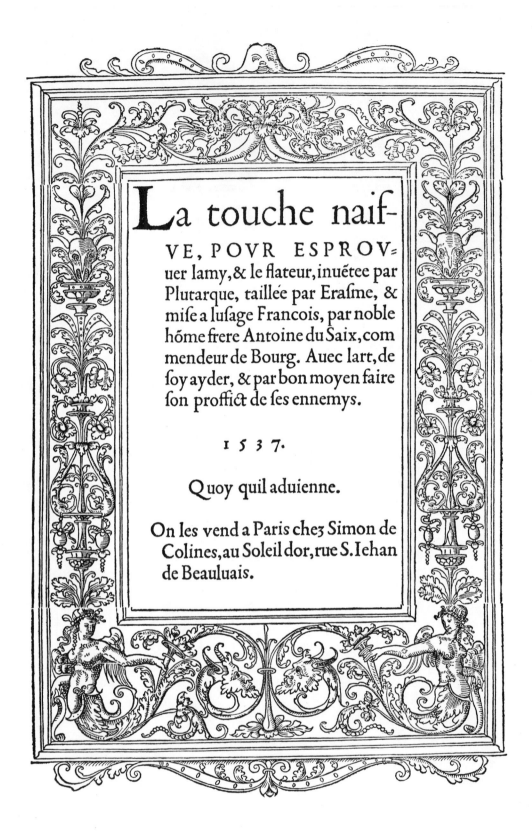

La touche naif-
VE, POVR ESPROV=
uer lamy, & le flateur, inuétee par
Plutarque, taillée par Erafme, &
mife a lufage Francois, par noble
hôme frere Antoine du Saix, com
mendeur de Bourg. Auec lart, de
foy ayder, & par bon moyen faire
fon proffict de fes ennemys.

1 5 3 7.

Quoy quil aduienne.

On les vend a Paris che3 Simon de
Colines, au Soleil dor, rue S. Iehan
de Beauluais.

PLATE 41. A four-piece title, school of Tory.   Used by de Colines, 1537.

ABBATTIMENTO
POETICO
del Diuino Aretino, et del
Beſtiale Albicante, occorſo
ſopra la guerra di Piemonte,
et la pace loro, celebrata
nella Academia de gli
Intronati à
Siena.

ESERNIVS

CVM

PACIDIANO

PLATE 42. A lively title used by F. Calvo, Milan, 1539.

Patere aut abstine.

Nul ne s'y frotte.

Lymage de Temerité.

✱ Temerité trop ieune sotte,
Sur vng cheual voltigé & trotte
Sans selle, sans resne, & sans bride,
Et sans aucir aucune guide,

PLATE 43. Pages from the *Hecatongraphie*. Printed by Denys Janot, Paris, 1543.

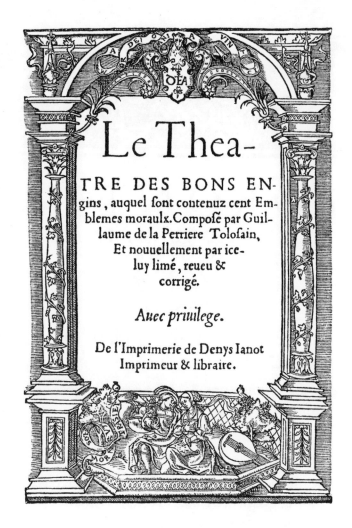

PLATE 44. Another Janot book of 1543. Tory influence is evident here and in Plate 43.

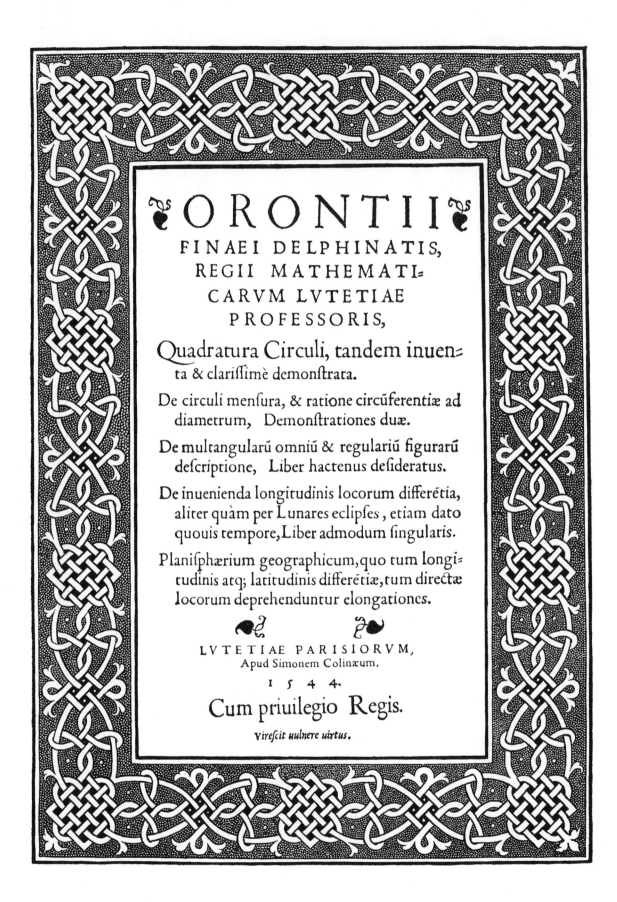

ORONTII
FINAEI DELPHINATIS,
REGII MATHEMATI=
CARVM LVTETIAE
PROFESSORIS,

Quadratura Circuli, tandem inuen=
ta & clariſſimè demonſtrata.

De circuli menſura, & ratione circúferentiæ ad
diametrum, Demonſtrationes duæ.

De multangularú omniú & regulariú figurarú
deſcriptione, Liber hactenus deſideratus.

De inuenienda longitudinis locorum differētia,
aliter quàm per Lunares eclipſes, etiam dato
quouis tempore, Liber admodum ſingularis.

Planiſphærium geographicum, quo tum longi=
tudinis atq; latitudinis differētiæ, tum directæ
locorum deprehenduntur elongationes.

LVTETIAE PARISIORVM,
Apud Simonem Colinæum.
1544.
Cum priuilegio Regis.

Vireſcit uulnere uirtus.

PLATE 45. A famous Oronce Finé border.   Printed by Simon de Colines.

IL LIBRO DEL CORTEGIANO
DEL CONTE BALDESSAR
CASTIGLIONE,

Nuouamente riſtampato ·

IN VENETIA, M· D· XLV·

PLATE 46. A late form of Aldus Manutius's device, used by his sons, Venice, 1545.

QVINTO LIBRO D'ARCHI-
TETTVRA DI SABASTIA-
NO SERLIO BOLOGNESE,

Nel quale se tratta de diuerse forme de Tempij sacri
secondo il costume Christiano, & al modo Antico.
A la serenissima Regina di Nauarra.

Traduict en Francois par Ian Martin, Secre-
taire de Monseigneur le Reuerendissime Cardinal de Lenoncourt.

A PARIS,
DE L'IMPRIMERIE DE MI-
CHEL DE VASCOSAN.
M. D. XLVII.
AVEC PRIVILEGE DV ·ROY.

PLATE 47. A title border by Sebastian Serlio, quite modern in its effect. 1547.

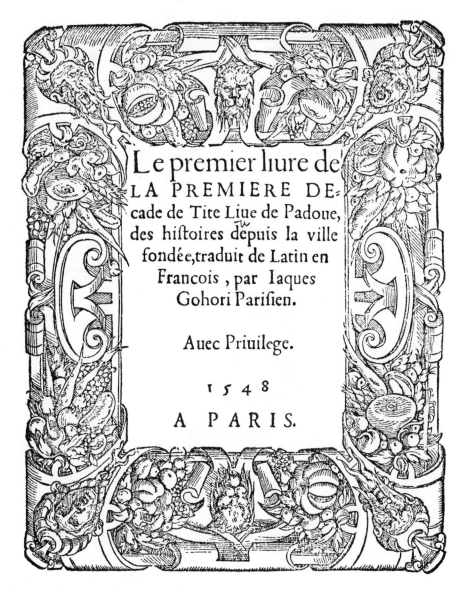

Le premier liure de
LA PREMIERE DE-
cade de Tite Liue de Padoue,
des hiftoires depuis la ville
fondée, traduit de Latin en
Francois, par Iaques
Gohori Parifien.

Auec Priuilege.

1548

A PARIS.

On le vend au fecond pillier de la grande
falle du Palais, par Arnould
l'Angelier.

PLATE 48. This title represents the Fontainebleau style. Paris, 1548.

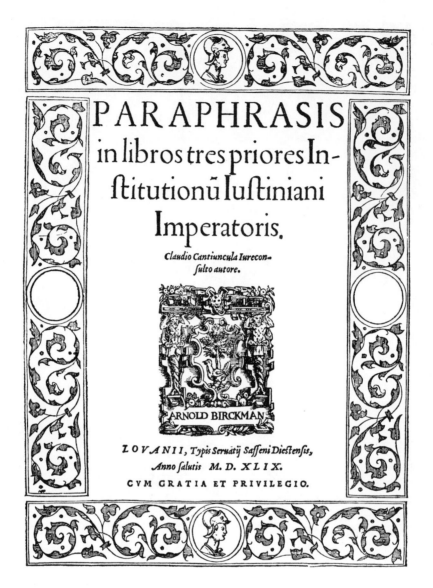

PLATE 49. Arabesque borders made their appearance about this time.   1549.

Des Aller= durchleuchtigstē

Großmechtigsten Keyser Carols deß

fünfften/ vnsers Allergenädigsten Herrn/ vnd jrer May. geliebten
Sone/ deß Printzen auß Hispanien/frölice glückselige Ankunfft gen Bintz/ den 22.
Augusti deß 1549. Jars. Wie auch jr Key. May. vñ sein Fürstlich Durchleuchtigkeit / von Frauw
Marien zu Vngern vnd Böhem Königin/Wittib/rc. vnd der Königin auß Franckreich/mit grossen
freuden/triumph/ köstlicheit vñ pracht empfangen worden. Dieweil aber ein Thurnier zu Fuß zuuor
zu Brüssel auff den andern tag nach jr Keys. May. glückseligen ankunfft/ gen Bintz außgeschrieben/
ist doch solcher/von wegen/daß die so thurnieren wolten/noch nicht aller ding fertig vnd gerüst
gewest/ auff den 24 tag gedachts Monats auffgeschoben / vnnd auff maß
vnd weiß gehalten / als desselben Außschreiben bedinget
vnd mitbringt/so von wort zu wort .
hernach volgt.

PLATE 50. Strapwork and arabesques in the German area.   1549.

STATVTI DELLA
Honoranda Vniuerſita' de Mercatanti della Inclita Citta' di Bologna Riformati l'Anno M. D. L.

Per Anſelmo Giaccarello.

PLATE 51. French influence on the Italian title-page. 1550.

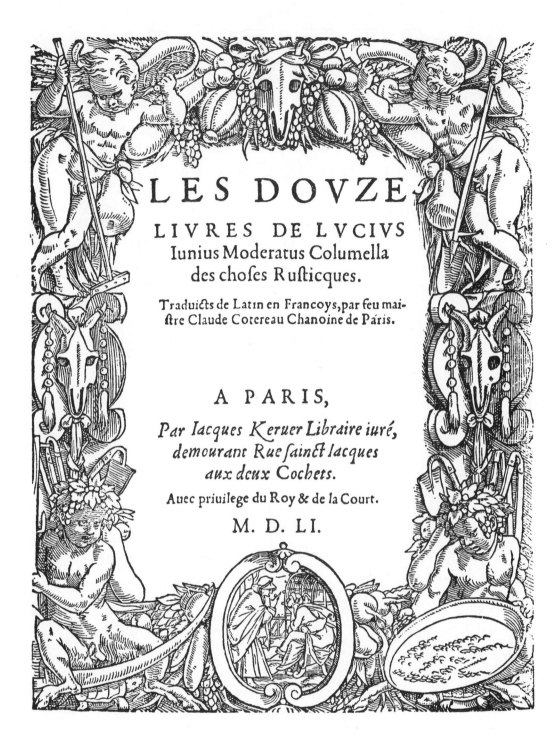

LES DOVZE
LIVRES DE LVCIVS
Iunius Moderatus Columella
des chofes Rufticques.

Traduicts de Latin en Francoys, par feu mai-
ftre Claude Cotereau Chanoine de Páris.

A PARIS,
Par Iacques Keruer Libraire iuré,
demourant Rue fainct Iacques
aux deux Cochets.
Auec priuilege du Roy & de la Court.
M. D. LI.

PLATE 52. The Fontainebleau manner again; the underlying feeling is
    baroque.   1551.

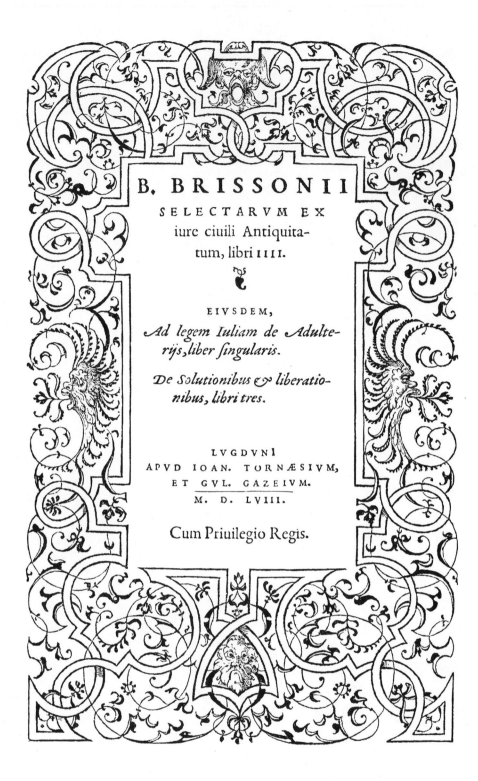

B. BRISSONII
SELECTARVM EX
iure ciuili Antiquita-
tum, libri IIII.

EIVSDEM,
Ad legem Iuliam de Adulte-
rijs, liber singularis.

De Solutionibus & liberatio-
nibus, libri tres.

LVGDVNI
APVD IOAN. TORNÆSIVM,
ET GVL. GAZEIVM.
M. D. LVIII.

Cum Priuilegio Regis.

PLATE 53. An arabesque border by Bernard Salomon. Printed by Jean de Tournes, 1558.

IMPERATORVM ROMA=
NORVM OMNIVM ORI
ENTALIVM ET OCCIDEN
TALIVM VERISSIMAE IMAGINES
EX ANTIQVIS NVMISMATIS QVAM
FIDELISSIME DELINEATAE.

ADDITA CVIVSQVE VITAE
DESCRIPTIONE EX
THESAVRO IACOBI STRADAE
ET PERBREVI ELOGIO VNIVSCV-
IVSQVE. CARMINE. QVOD QVASI
EPITOME EST HISTORIAE. AD
IVVANDAM MEMORIAM.

TIGVRI EX OFFICINA ANDREAE
GESNERI. ANNO
1559.

PLATE 54. Scroll-bordered titles relate to the architecture of the time.   1559.

PLATE 55. The title-page of a book about lace. Also used at Lyons around 1560.

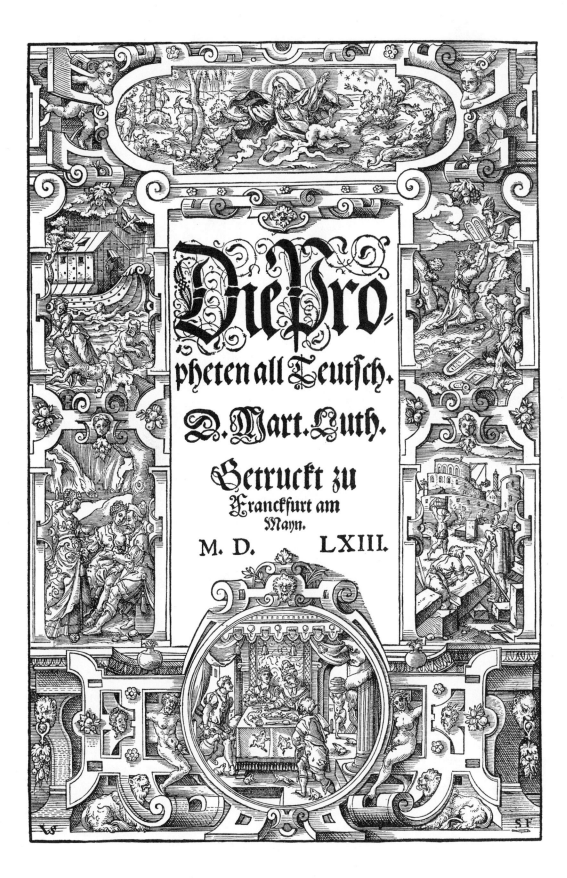

PLATE 56. A title by Virgil Solis for the noted publisher Sigmund Feyerabend, 1563.

PLATE 57. Another Feyerabend title by the master Jost Amman, 1568.

LIVRE
DE POVRTRAITVRE DE
MAISTRE IEAN COVSIN
PEINTRE ET GEOMETRIEN
TRES-EXCELLENT.

Contenant par vne facile instruction, plusieurs plans & figures de toutes les parties separees du corps humain: ensemble les figures entieres, tant d'homes
que de femmes, & de petits enfans: venés de front, de profil, & de
dos, auec les proportions, mesures, & dimansions d'icelles, &
certaines regles pourra ourcir par art toutes lesdites figures: fort vtile & necessaire aux Peintres, Statuaires,
Architectes, Orfeures, Brodeurs, Menusiers, &
generalement a tous ceux qui ayment l'art
de Peinture & de Sculpture.

A Paris chez Iean le Clerc, rue S. Iean de Latran, à la Sale-
mandre Royale. Auec priuilege du Roy.

PLATE 58. Probably the work of Jean Cousin the Younger. 1571.

IN STVDIO-
SORVM GRATIAM A
MENDIS OMNIBVS
probè expurgatorum.

PARS SECVNDA.

M. D. *LXXII.*

Franҫofůrti ad
Mænům.

PLATE 59. Woodcut titles became more and more intricate. Jost Amman, 1572.

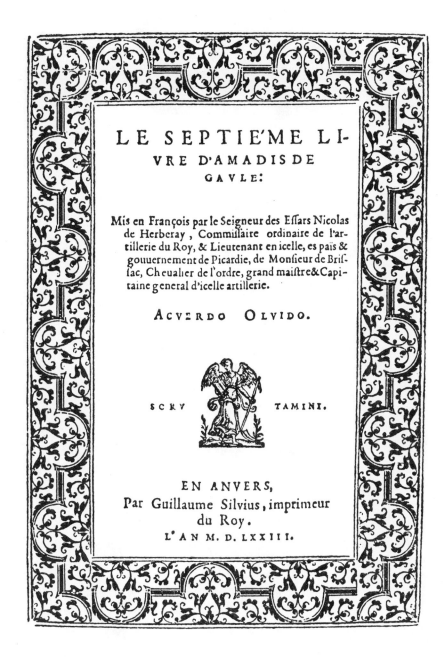

PLATE 60. A title border made from typographic arabesque units. Antwerp, 1573.

¶HISTORIA BRE-
uis Thomæ Walsingham,
ab Edwardo primo, ad
Henricum quintum.

LONDINI
Excusum apud Henricum
Binneman Typographum.
sub insigno Syrenis.

ANNO DOMINI
1574.

PLATE 61. These framework titles were much used in England at this period.

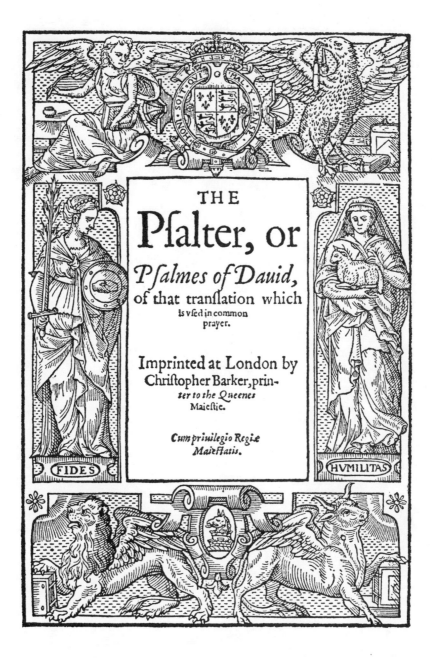

PLATE 62. "Compartment" is the bibliographical name for these frame
titles.   1579.

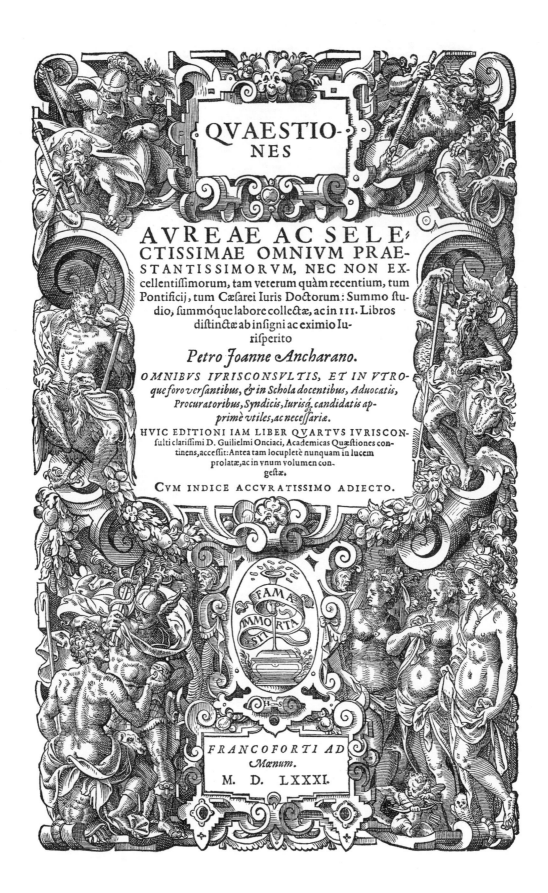

QVAESTIO-NES

AVREAE AC SELE-CTISSIMAE OMNIVM PRAE-STANTISSIMORVM, NEC NON EX-cellentiſſimorum, tam veterum quàm recentium, tum Pontificij, tum Cæſarei Iuris Doctorum: Summo ſtudio, ſummóque labore collectæ, ac in III. Libros diſtinctæ ab inſigni ac eximio Iuriſperito
Petro Joanne Ancharano.

OMNIBVS IVRISCONSVLTIS, ET IN VTRO-que foro verſantibus, & in Schola docentibus, Aduocatis, Procuratoribus, Syndicis, Iurisq̃ candidatis ap-primè vtiles, ac neceſſariæ.

HVIC EDITIONI IAM LIBER QVARTVS IVRISCON-ſulti clariſſimi D. Guilielmi Onciaci, Academicas Quæſtiones continens, acceſſit: Antea tam locupletè nunquam in lucem prolatæ, ac in vnum volumen con-geſtæ.

CVM INDICE ACCVRATISSIMO ADIECTO.

FAMA IMMORTA STI

FRANCOFORTI AD Mœnum.
M. D. LXXXI.

PLATE 63. One more of the fantastic Amman designs for Sigmund Feyerabend. 1581.

THE

Nevve Teſtament

of our Lord Ieſus
Chriſt,

*Conferred diligently with the Greeke, and
beſt approued tranſlations in diuers
languages.*

Imprinted at London by Chriſtopher
Barker, printer to the Queenes moſt
excellent Maieſtie.
1583.

Cum gratia & priuilegio
Regiæ Maieſtatis.

C.   B.

PROVERBES. XXX.
5 Euery word of God is pure : he is a ſhield to thoſe
that truſt in him.
6 Put nothing vnto his wordes, leaſt he reproue
thee, and thou be found a liar.

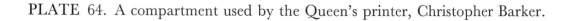

PLATE 64. A compartment used by the Queen's printer, Christopher Barker.

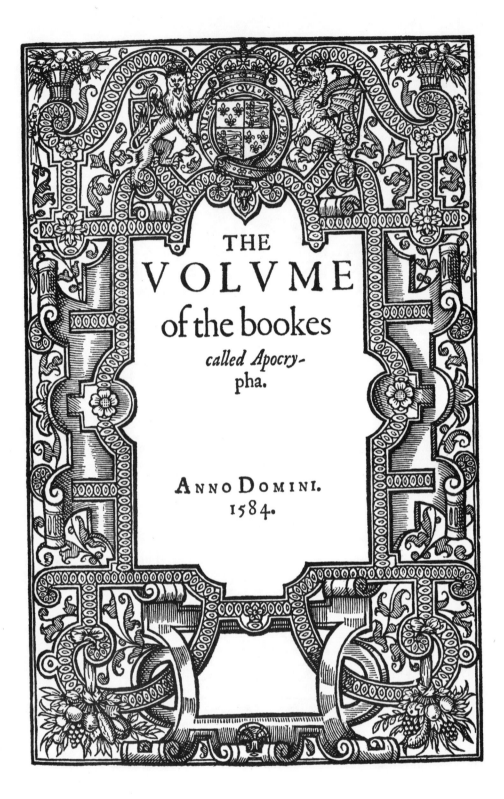

THE
VOLVME
of the bookes
called Apocry-
pha.

ANNO DOMINI.
1584.

PLATE 65. Compartments were often used for many different books, slightly altered.

PLATE 66. Title border by Tobias Stimmer, another famous cutter of this
   time.   1588.

M. TVLLII
CICERONIS
OPERA OMNIA·

Præter hactenus vulgatam *Dionysij Lambini* edi-
tionem, accesserunt D. GOTHOFREDI
IC. Notę: in queis

Variæ lectiones propè infinitę: *Synopses* generales & specia
les singulis vel libris vel paginis adiectæ : *Ciceronis loca præ-
cipua* & difficiliora, inter se primò: alijs deinde authoribu
Grammaticis, Rhetoribus. Poetis, Historicis, Iurisconsultis
maximè collata : vt & *Formulæ* quæ ad ius, leges, senatuf
consulta & actiones pertinent explicatę.

*Index Generalis breuitate & arte summa compositus
prater superiora adiectus est.*

LVGDVNI,
Sumptibus Sybillæ à Porta.
M. D. LXXXVIII.

*Cum priuilegio Cæsareæ Maiestatis, & Christianiff.
Galliarum & Polon. Regis.*

PLATE 67. A fine architectural frame by the unknown master G. L. Lyons,
1588.

PLATE 68. Decorative title borders that belong to the 1560–1600 period.

PLATE 69. Frames and pieces signed A. F.   Used in the period
between 1590 and 1620.

II. The Etched or Engraved Title

II. The Etched or Engraved Title

The first engraved title appeared in England, actually a most unlikely place. It was apparently the work of a Dutch engraver. This page, the title to the 1545 London edition of Thomas Geminus's anatomy (70), is the first example in this section. S. H. Steinberg considers it the beginning of an aberration in the art of the book in which the woodcuts and metal-cuts that had worked so well with type were largely displaced by the intaglio process for decoration and illustration. It is not necessary to become involved in controversial aspects of this problem; it is an historic fact that engraving and etching became the dominant methods for producing the titles and illustrations of fine books. There was an attraction about the technical possibilities of this process for wider tonal range and greater depth, that allowed it to supplant the older technique. Of course woodcutting continued, but with greatly reduced frequency and quality; it did not become popular again until the 1830's in France and England, after the appearance of Thomas Bewick and the development of wood engraving.

Another method of making title-page borders and decorations may be mentioned at this point: this entailed the use of cast typographic ornament such as *fleurons*, *Röschen*, and printers' flowers. The first striking employment of such ornament was in the book *Arte de ben morire*, printed by Giovanni and Alberto Alvise in Verona, 1478. This method, which provided a kind of do-it-yourself opportunity for the printer, was used for the less pretentious books. A few such titles have been included throughout the three sections of the present work to remind the reader of this most interesting area of title-page design.

Title designs were also improvised by combining pieces of woodcut ornament already on hand. The book printer had to be resourceful and he used, in all sorts of ways, whatever material he had. Very few of these titles are shown here for the simple reason that they are most often not particularly good. In most instances these pieced borders have been noted as such in the plate captions.

Many complete blocks for illustrations were used over and over again; they traveled from one country to another, served for all kinds of books. Sometimes the later use was as successful as the original one, but most often there were disfiguring alterations; then, too, the blocks became always the worse for wear. Because of the greater technical difficulties of altering etched and engraved titles, these were not so frequently re-used as the headpieces, tailpieces, and vignettes that were revived wherever they seemed to fit.

In general, the seventeenth century was not a good one for the art of the book. Quality declined in France and in the German area; England suffered under the Stuart censorship and good craftsmen and materials had to be imported. But we may see in this period the gradual introduction of the engraving and etching processes and their eventual supremacy. The impetus came largely from the Dutch area, beginning with such engravers as Hubert Goltzius, who was already at work in the latter part of the sixteenth century. His *Sicilia et Magna Graecia* title (71) is decidedly different in effect from any of the woodcut titles in the first section of the present book. The art of the goldsmith and the abilities of all engravers in metal were also brought to the service of the title-page.

Some of the plates show the efforts of these craftsmen to display their abilities as designers; they created their own title-pages for their specimen books of ornament and pattern. Pages of the work of the writing-masters Jan van den Velde (83) and Jodocus Hondius (90), the lockmaker Hugues Brisville (105), and the decorative painter Johann Daniel Preissler (116) indicate the trend. Whole families of engravers and etchers grew up to take over the task of ornament on metal and in the illustrated book. They worked with designs created by draftsmen—engraving, etching, and printing them. As in the period of the woodcut, designer and engraver were often one and the same person. An enormous quantity of work was produced: architectural texts, books of ornament of all kinds, whole volumes and portfolios of city views, battle scenes, and reproductions of paintings and portraits were printed by the engraving process.

The engraving process was refined through the seventeenth century, attaining an ever more expert level. The style passed through the baroque into the rococo, becoming more meticulous in detail and finish. Especially in France during the reigns of Louis XIV and Louis XV there was a superb evolution of book ornament, of the book as a whole. Here, in this final phase, the work of engraver-artists such as Charles Eisen (119, 122, 127), Hubert François Gravelot (128), and Clément Pierre Marillier (133, 136) brought to its brilliant close the long development of French taste and style that had affected all the countries of Europe.

The peculiar culture, the mode of life of France, could be carried no further; the era came to an end in the cataclysm of the French Revolution. An important contributing factor was the growing industrial revolution, which was bringing a new class in society to power. The changed outlook in thought and in aesthetics that had been developing through the reigns of Louis XV and Louis XVI repudiated the culture of the Bourbons and abandoned rococo style. A new epoch was marked in the development of European art and in the course of history. For a time book decoration and illustration of the sort familiar for a century was practically forgotten. In England John Baskerville, whose work preceded the debacle of the Revolution, generally used no decoration on his title-pages; in Italy Giambattista Bodoni's severe titles bore little or no ornament. Both men had great influence on the appearance of the fine book throughout Europe. It was well into the nineteenth century before the decorative title came into widespread use again; but the engraved title was never to regain the popularity it had enjoyed in the past.

VICTORIA.

IVSTICIA.

PRVDENTIA.

DIEV ET MON DROYT.

COMPENDIOSA
totius Anatomiæ delineatio, ære
exarata: per Thomam Geminum.
LONDINI.

PLATE 70. Earliest engraved title, possibly by a Dutch artist. London, 1545.

PLATE 71. Title by Hubert Goltzius, printer and engraver of Bruges. 1576.

PLATE 72. Titles to books of designs for goldsmiths, Nürnberg. Johann
Sibmacher, 1599; Georg Wechter, 1579.

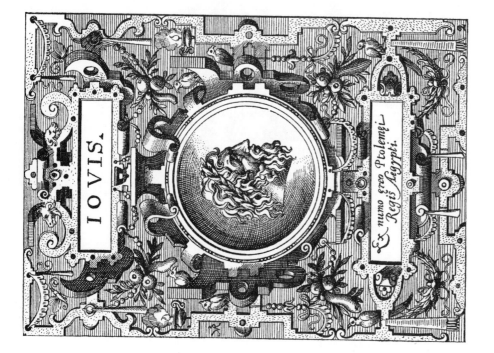

PLATE 73. Facsimiles from a book of medals.   Abraham Ortelius, Antwerp
and Brussels.

A CON
CENT OF
Scripture
by
H: BROVGHTON

עור עשׁו

PLATE 74. An engraved title by William Rogers.   London, 1590.

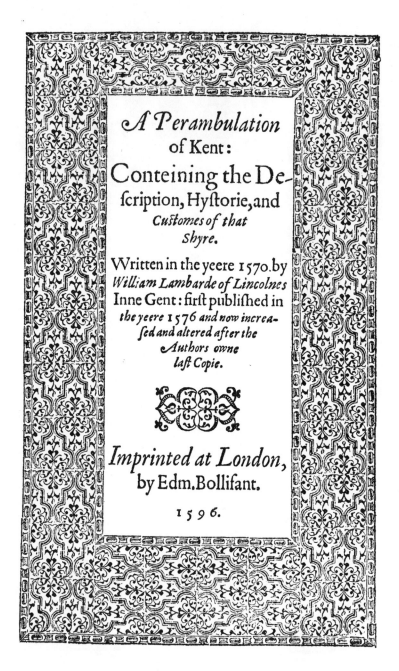

A Perambulation
of Kent:
Conteining the De-
scription, Hystorie, and
Customes of that
Shyre.

Written in the yeere 1570. by
William Lambarde of Lincolnes
Inne Gent: first published in
the yeere 1576 and now increa-
sed and altered after the
Authors owne
last Copie.

Imprinted at London,
by Edm. Bollifant.
1596.

PLATE 75. Printers' flowers. These designs came to England from Lyons
and Antwerp. 1596.

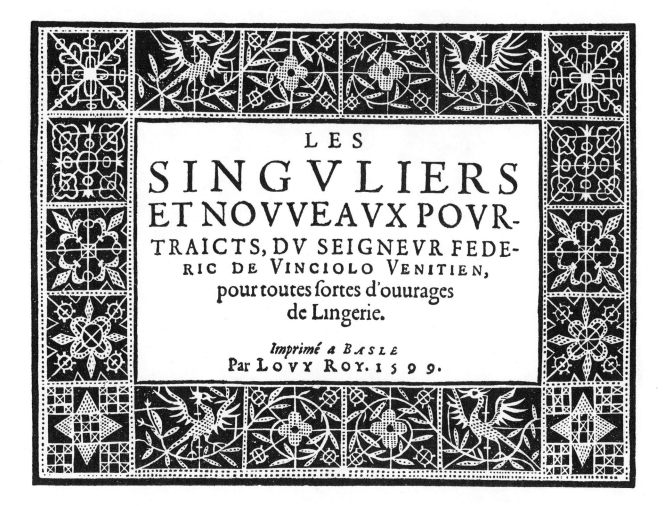

LES SINGVLIERS

ET NOVVEAVX POVR-
TRAICTS, DV SEIGNEVR FEDE-
RIC DE VINCIOLO VENITIEN,
pour toutes sortes d'ouurages
de Lingerie.

Imprimé a BASLE
Par LOVY ROY. 1 5 9 9.

PLATE 76. Title of a book about lace. Basel, 1599.

PLATE 77. Title-page engraved by Crispin van de Passe the Elder. Cologne, 1601.

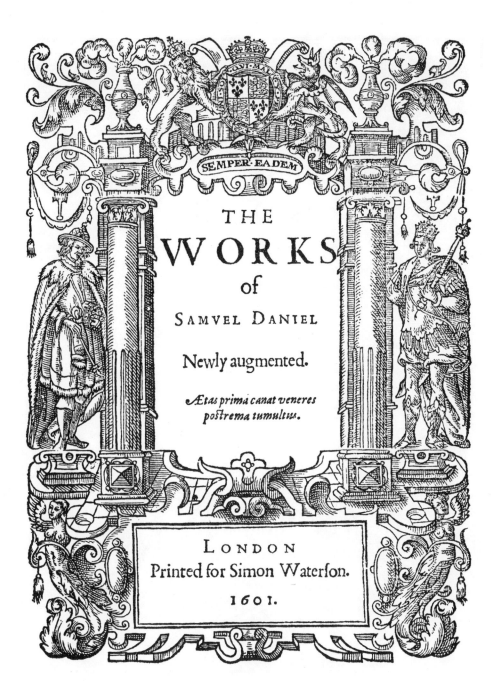

SEMPER·EADEM

THE
WORKS
of
SAMVEL DANIEL

Newly augmented.

Ætas primá canat veneres postrema tumultus.

LONDON
Printed for Simon Waterson.
1601.

PLATE 78. The woodcut border continued in use in England. London, 1601.

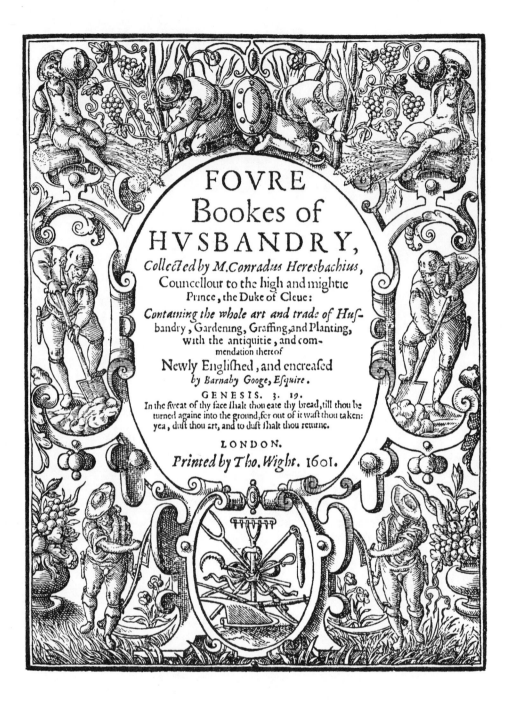

FOVRE
Bookes of
HVSBANDRY,
Collected by M. Conradus Heresbachius,
Councellour to the high and mightie
Prince, the Duke of Cleue:
Containing the whole art and trade of Hus-
bandry, Gardening, Graffing, and Planting,
with the antiquitie, and com-
mendation thereof
Newly Englished, and encreased
by Barnaby Googe, Esquire.
GENESIS. 3. 19.
In the sweat of thy face shalt thou eate thy bread, till thou be
turned againe into the ground, for out of it wast thou taken:
yea, dust thou art, and to dust shalt thou returne.
LONDON.
Printed by Tho. Wight. 1601.

PLATE 79. Influence of French and Dutch design.   London, 1601.

PLATE 80. The work of an unknown master for Jean de Tournes.   Lyons-
Geneva, 1602.

THE
GENERALL HISTORIE
of the Turkes, from The first
beginning of that Nation to the rising
of the Othoman Familie: with
all the notable expeditions
of the Christian
Princes against
them.

Together with

THE LIVES AND CON=
quests of the OTHOMAN
Kings and Emperours

Faithfullie collected out of the
best Histories, both auntient and mo=
derne, and digested into one continu=
at Historie untill this present
yeare 1603:

By RICHARD KNOLLES

LONDON:
Printed by Adam Islip. 1603.

Laurence Johnson. Sculpsit

PLATE 81. Title engraved by Laurence Johnson.   London, 1603.

PLATE 82. A title by the Nürnberg designer, Johann Sibmacher. 1604.

PLATE 83. Title for the writing-master's book of Jan van den Velde.
Rotterdam, 1605.

Newes

GRADESCA
Büchlein
Durch Lucas Kilian
Burger Jn Augspurg
vñd
Kupfferstecher
gradiert vnd an tag.
geben

MDC VII·

PLATE 84. A title-page engraved by the best of all the Kilians, Lucas Kilian.
Augsburg, 1607.

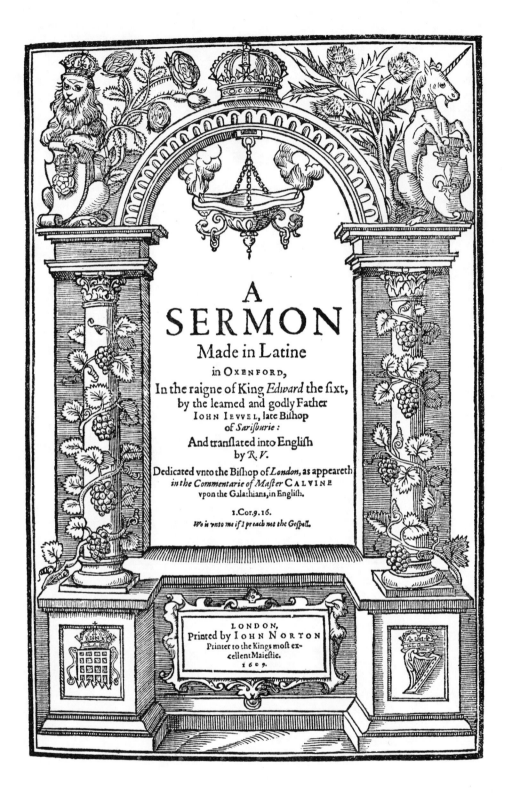

PLATE 85. A favorite type of woodcut compartment. London, 1609.

Mulciber in Troiam;

pro Troia stabat Apollo;

HOMER
Prince of
Poets:

Translated accord=
ing to the Greeke,
in
twelue Bookes of
his Iliads,
By
Geo: Chapman

Qui Nil molitur
Inepte

Achilles

Hector

At London printed for Samuel Macham   Will: Hole sculp:

PLATE 86. Title for the Chapman *Iliad*, engraved by William Hole about 1610.

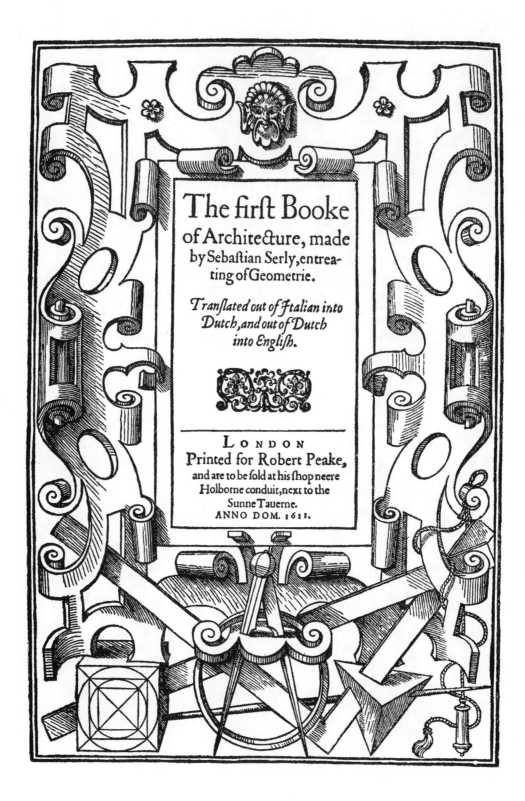

The first Booke
of Architecture, made
by Sebastian Serly, entrea-
ting of Geometrie.

Translated out of Italian into
Dutch, and out of Dutch
into English.

LONDON
Printed for Robert Peake,
and are to be fold at his fhop neere
Holborne conduit, next to the
Sunne Tauerne.
ANNO DOM. 1611.

PLATE 87. A much-traveled block; used earlier at Antwerp and Basel. London.

THE WORKES OF Mr SAM. HIERON late Pastor of Modbury in DEUON

IOHN . 5 . 55.
He was a burning and a shining light

LONDON
Printed by William
Stansby and Iohn
Beale

HUMILITIE

FAITH

S. MATTHEW.

S. MARKE.

S. LUKE.

S. IOHN.

R: Elstracke sculp.

PLATE 88. Used in London about 1614. The engraver, Elstrack, was of
Flemish parentage.

MIRIFICI

Logarithmorum
Canonis descriptio,

Ejusque usus, in utraque
Trigonometria; ut etiam in
omni Logistica Mathematica,
Amplissimi, Facillimi, &
expeditissimi explicatio.

Authore ac Inventore,
IOANNE NEPERO,
Barone Merchistonii,
&c. Scoto.

EDINBURGI,
Ex officinâ ANDREÆ HART
Bibliopólæ, cIↃ. Dc. XIV.

PLATE 89. Edinburgh, 1614.   The design appeared in slightly different form in London.

PLATE 90. Pages from a writing book. Jodocus Hondius, Amsterdam, 1614.

AN
A&t for the graunt
of one entier Subfidie by
the Temporaltie.

DVBLIN.
Imprinted by Iohn Franckton Printer
to the Kings moft excellent Maiefty
Anno 1615.

PLATE 91. A compartment of the niche type. Used in Dublin, 1615.

A

BOOKE OF SVNDRY
DRAVGHTES,
Principaly ferving for Glafiers:
And not Impertinent for
Plafterers, and Gardiners:
be fides fundry other
profeffions.
WHEREVNTO IS AN-
nexed the manner how to anniel
in Glas:
And alfo the true forme of
the Fornace, and the fe-
cretes thereof.
LONDON Printed in Shoolane,
at the figne of the Faulcon
by Walter Dight. 1615.

PLATE 92. Title of a book for glaziers.   London, 1615–1616.

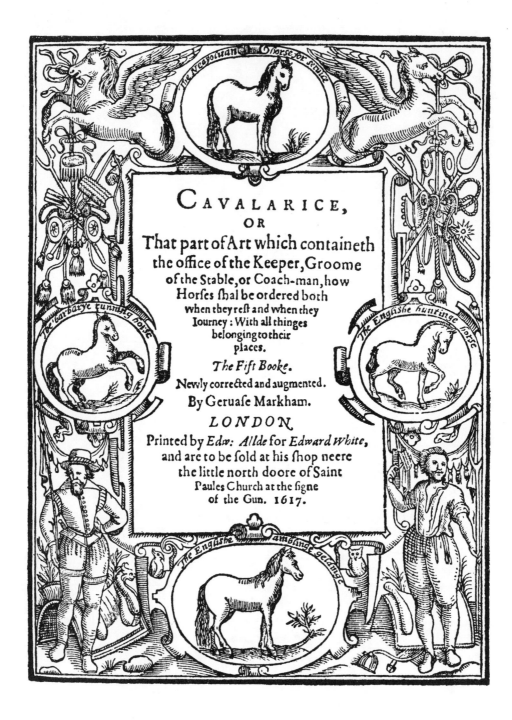

PLATE 93. Title-page of a book for keepers, grooms, coachmen. London.

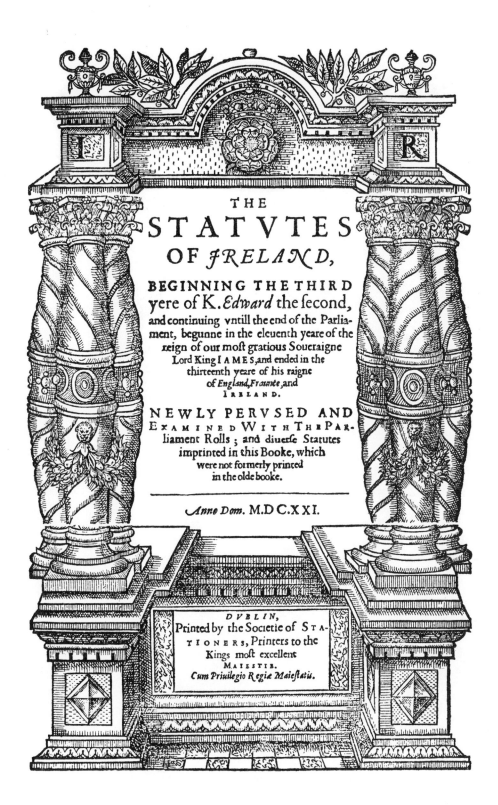

THE
STATVTES
OF IRELAND,

BEGINNING THE THIRD
yere of K. *Edward* the second,
and continuing vntill the end of the Parlia-
ment, begunne in the eleuenth yeare of the
reign of our moſt gratious Soueraigne
Lord King I A M E S, and ended in the
thirteenth yeare of his raigne
of *England, Fraunce,* and
I R E L A N D.

NEWLY PERVSED AND
E X A M I N E D W I T H T H E Par-
liament Rolls ; and diuerſe Statutes
imprinted in this Booke, which
were not formerly printed
in the olde booke.

Anno Dom. M.DC.XXI.

DVBLIN,
Printed by the Societie of S T A-
T I O N E R S, Printers to the
Kings moſt excellent
M A I E S T I E.
Cum Priuilegio Regiæ Maieſtatis.

PLATE 94. A title with curious columns.   Dublin, 1621.

œuures
de
Philibert
de
l'Orme.

A PARIS,
Chez Regnavld Chavdiere,
ruë S. Iacques, à l'Efcu de Florence.

M·DC·XXVI·

PLATE 95. From a facsimile of an engraved book-title. Paris, 1626.

THE
GVNNER
SHEWING THE
WHOLE PRACTISE
OF *ARTILLERY*:

With all the Appurtenances
thereunto belonging.

Together with the ma-
king of exrraordinarie Arti-
ficiall *Fire-workes*, as well for
Pleasure and Triumphes, as
for Warre and Seruice.

Written by ROBERT NORTON,
one of his Maiesties Gunners
and *Enginiers*.

Printed at London by *A. M.* for *Humphrey*
Robinson, and are to be sold at the three Pidgeons
in *Pauls-Church yard.* 1628.

PLATE 96. Cannons as columns; the title of an artillery manual. London.

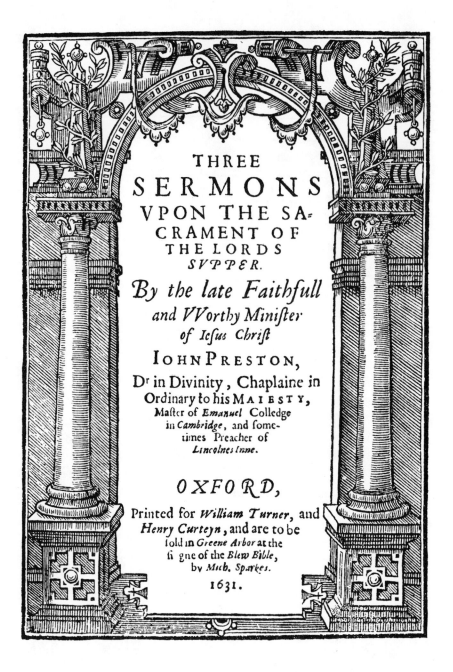

THREE
SERMONS
VPON THE SA-
CRAMENT OF
THE LORDS
SVPPER.

By the late Faithfull
and VVorthy Miniſter
of Ieſus Chriſt

IOHN PRESTON,

Dr in Divinity, Chaplaine in
Ordinary to his MAIESTY,
Maſter of *Emanuel* Colledge
in *Cambridge*, and ſome-
times Preacher of
Lincolnes Inne.

OXFORD,

Printed for *William Turner*, and
Henry Curteyn, and are to be
ſold in *Greene Arbor* at the
ſigne of the *Blew Bible*,
by *Mich. Sparkes.*
1631.

PLATE 97. A typical columned title of this period. Oxford, 1631.

HERE FOLLOVVETH
CERTAINE PATTERNES

OF *Cut-workes*: and but once Printed before.

Alſo ſundry ſorts of Spots, as Flowers, Birds and Fiſhes &c. and will fitly ſerve to be wrought, ſome with Gould, ſome with Silke, and ſome with Crewell, or otherwyſe as your pleaſure.

LONDON, Pinted in Shoe-lane, at the
figne of the Faulcon, by *Richard Shorleyker.* 1632.

PLATE 98. A framed title made of pieces. London, 1632.

LIVRE DE
FLEVRS & DE
FEVLLIES POVR
SERVIR A L'ART D'OR-
FEVERIE INVANTE
PAR FRANCOIS LE
FEBVRE MAISTRE
ORFEVRE A PARIS

BALTAZAR MONCORNET
FECIT ET EXCVDIT

F. L. D. Ciartres
excud

Auec Priuilege
1635

PLATE 99. Engraved title showing Callot influence. 1635.

PLATE 100. A title in the older cutting process.   Dublin, 1636.

A

COLLECTION
of sundry Statutes, frequent
in use: With Notes in the Mar-
gent and References to the Book cases
and Books of Entries and Regi-
sters, where they be treated of.

Together with an Abridgement of
the residue which be expired, re-
pealed, altered, and worn out of use,
or doe concern private Persons, Places, or
Things, and not the whole Common-wealth.

Also a necessary Table, or Kalender, is an-
nexed hereunto, expressing in Titles the
most materiall Branches of those Statutes in use, and practice

By FARDINANDO PULTON
of Lincolnes Inne, Esquire

AND
Now in this last Impression the faults
in the Table exactly corrected
and amended.

LONDON,
Printed by *M. Flesher* and *R. Young,* Assignes of *I. More*
Esquire. 1640.   *Cum Privilegio*

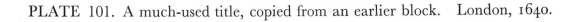

PLATE 101. A much-used title, copied from an earlier block.   London, 1640.

The text in the central medallion reads:

Nieu
WAPEN
BOEXKEN
van
M le Blon
1649

PLATE 102. Facsimiles from the book of crests by Michel le Blond. 1649.

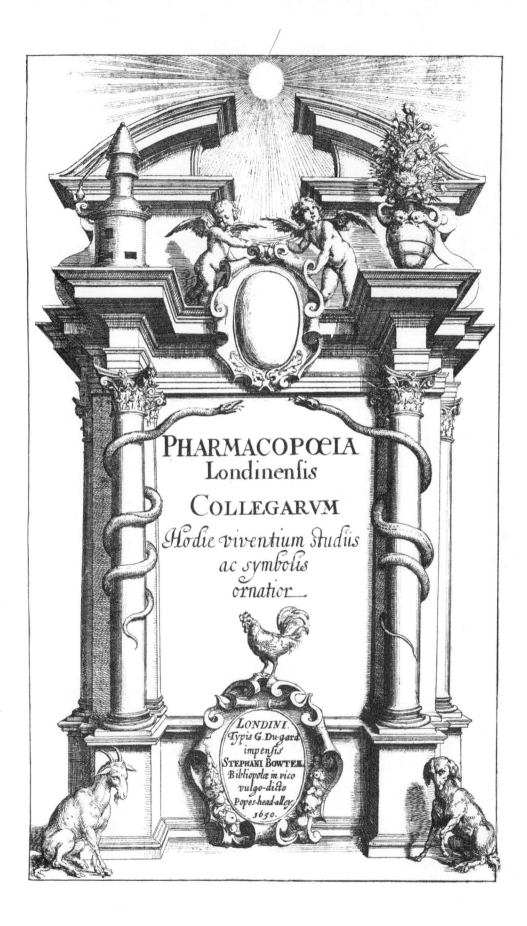

PLATE 103. Typical architectural title, suggesting a portal. London, 1650.

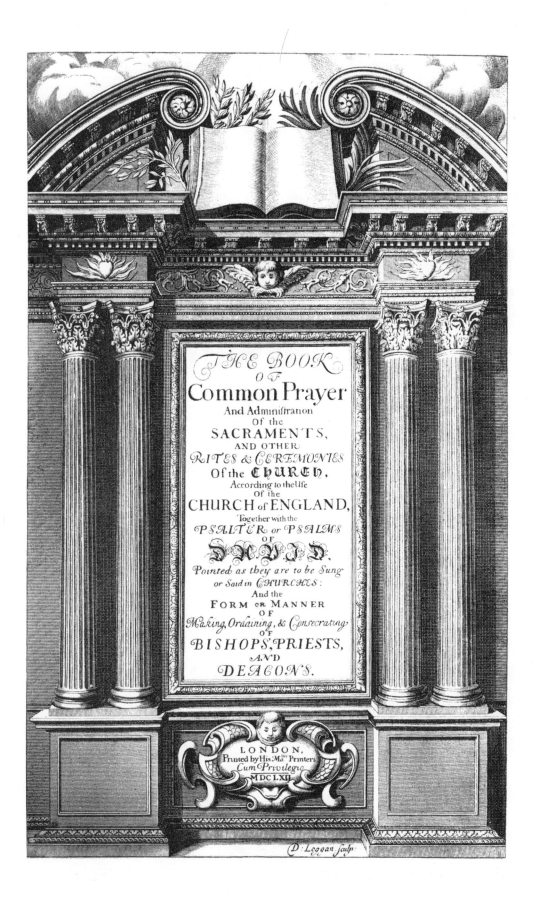

PLATE 104. Copied from an earlier title; engraved by David Loggan.
London, 1662.

PLATE 105. Title and page from a book of designs for locks. Hugues Brisville,
Paris.

PLATE 106. Title-page for a book of writing hands.   Nürnberg, 1665.

ÆSOP's
FABLES
With his Life
In English French & Latine
The English by Tho. Philipott Esq
The French and Latine
by Rob: Codrington M.A.
Illustrated with
one hundred and ten
SCULPTURES
By Francis Barlow
And
Are Sold at his House
The Golden Eagle
In New-Street,
near Shoo-Lane.
1665

PLATE 107. A title by Francis Barlow, a painter of birds and animals. 1665.

PLATE 108. Engraved title of a manual for pilots. London, about 1672.

Printed for Tho. Dring at ý. Corner of Chancery lane in Fleetstreet. 1675.

PLATE 109. From a book on agriculture. Title engraved by Frederik van
Hove. 1675.

PLATE 110. The plate for this 1683 title was also used in several earlier states.

Nouueaux Liure
d'Ornements, Pour Lutillitée
des Sculpteurs, et Orfeures
Jnuenté et Grauée a La Haye
Par D. Marot. Architecte de
Guilliaume III Roy d'Angleterre
fait auec Preuillege
des Etats Generaux des Prouinces Vnie
Et des Etats d'Hollande et de
West Frise.

Marot fec exc Priuil des Etats generaux des Prouinces Vnie et d'hollande et West frise

PLATE 111. The work of Daniel Marot; dedicated to William of Orange.

PLATE 112. From a book of designs by Friedrich Jacob Morisson; engraved by Pfeffel.

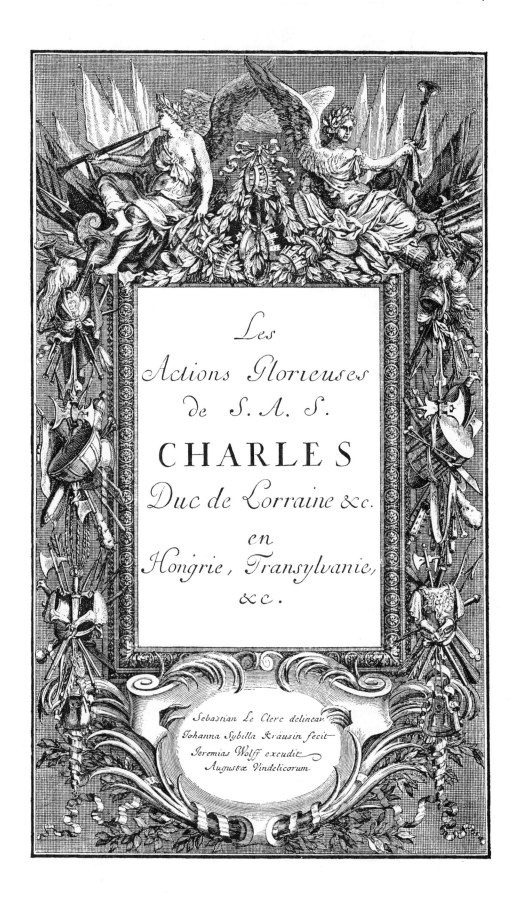

Les
Actions Glorieuses
de S. A. S.
CHARLES
Duc de Lorraine &c.
en
Hongrie, Transylvanie,
&c.

Sebastian Le Clerc delineav.
Iohanna Sybilla Kräusin fecit
Ieremias Wolff excudit
Augustæ Vindelicorum.

PLATE 113. Engraved from the design of Sebastien Le Clerc, turn of the century.

PLATE 114. From a cartouche by Turreau, sculptor and decorative draftsman. About 1717.

PLATE 115. Facsimile of title, head- and tail-pieces by Bernard Picart. About
1730.

F.

E.

PLATE 116. Designs from *Orthographia* by Johann Daniel Preissler. Nürnberg.

COURONNEMENT DE TREMEAU AVEC TROPHÉE DE SCULPTURE

Dessein de la traverse d'en bas.

Echelle de   1   2   3   *4 Pieds*

B. inv. et f.   64

PLATE 117. Plate from a book on architecture, Jacques François Blondel. About 1737.

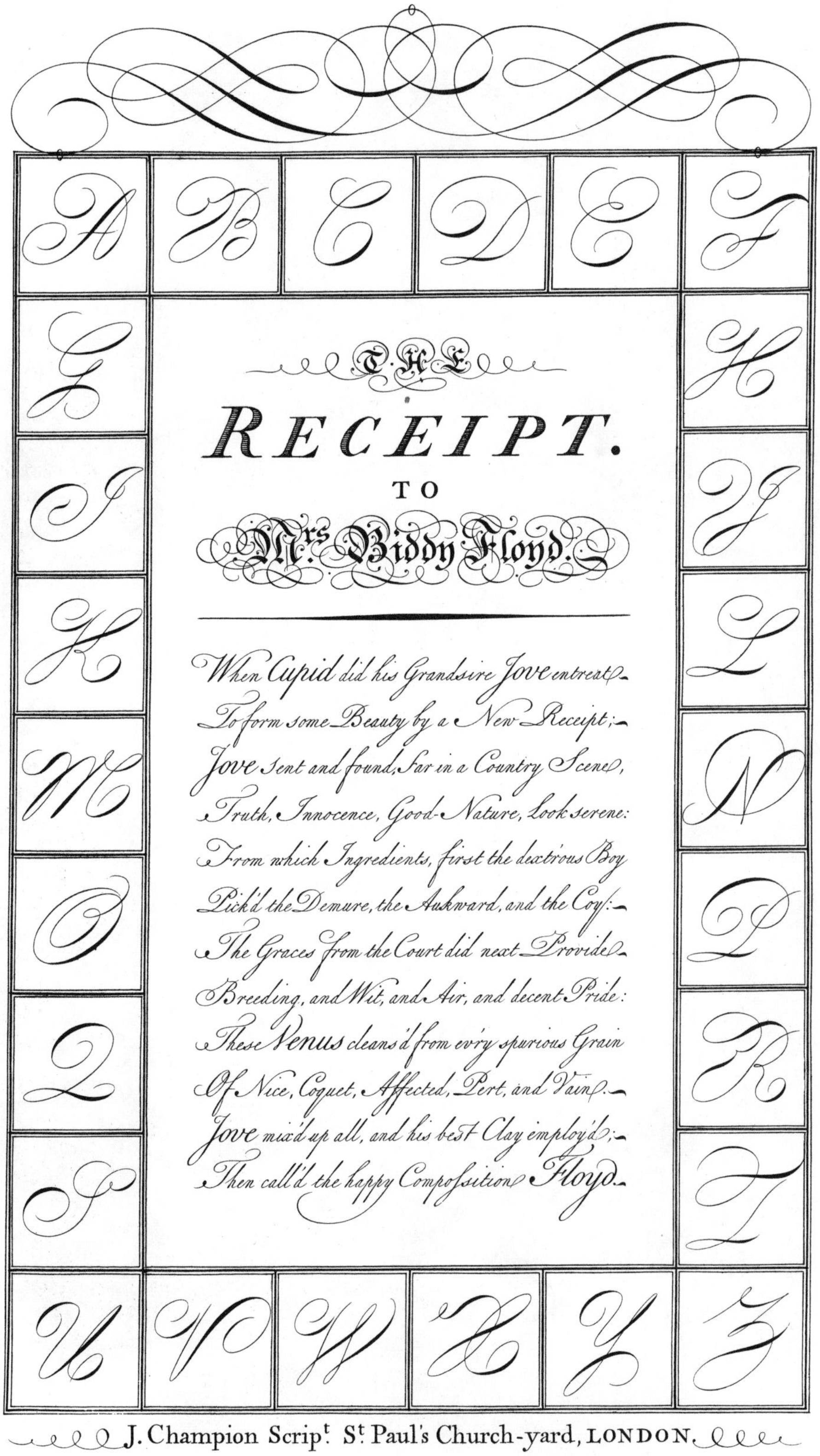

A B C D E F
G H
I J
K L
M N
O P
Q R
S T
U V W X Y Z

THE
RECEIPT.
TO
Mrs Biddy Floyd.

When Cupid did his Grandsire JOVE entreat
To form some Beauty by a New Receipt;
Jove sent and found, Far in a Country Scene,
Truth, Innocence, Good-Nature, Look serene:
From which Ingredients, first the dextrous Boy
Pick'd the Demure, the Aukward, and the Coy:
The Graces from the Court did next Provide
Breeding, and Wit, and Air, and decent Pride:
These Venus cleans'd from ev'ry spurious Grain
Of Nice, Coquet, Affected, Pert, and Vain.
Jove mix'd up all, and his best Clay employ'd;
Then call'd the happy Compofsition Floyd.

J. Champion Script St. Paul's Church-yard, LONDON.

PLATE 118. Page from George Bickham's *Universal Penman*. 1743.*

* Reprinted by Dover Publications, Inc., in 1954.

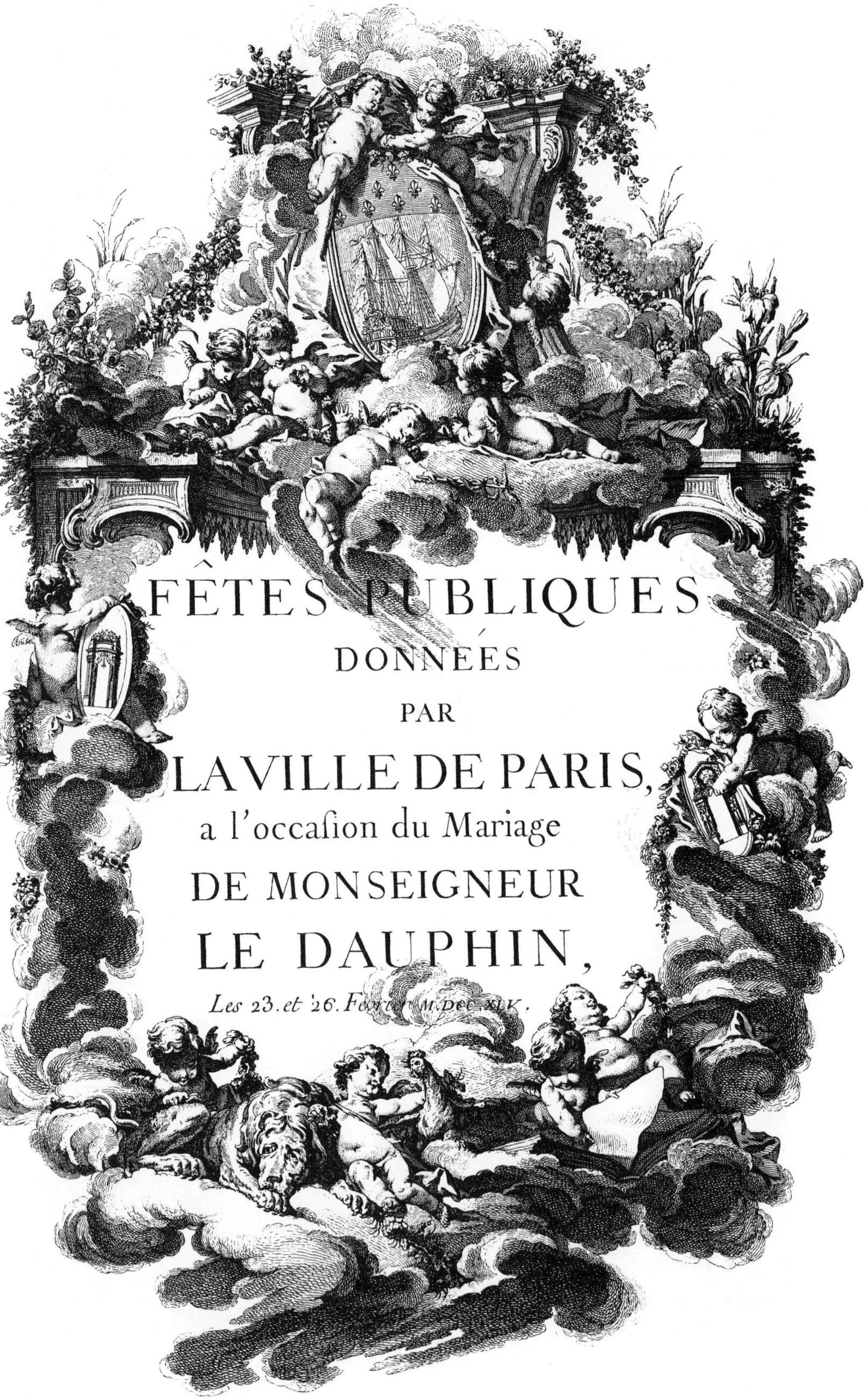

FÊTES PUBLIQUES

DONNÉES

PAR

LA VILLE DE PARIS,

a l'occasion du Mariage

DE MONSEIGNEUR

LE DAUPHIN,

Les 23. et 26. Février M.DCC.XLV.

PLATE 119. Engraved title design by Charles Eisen. 1745.

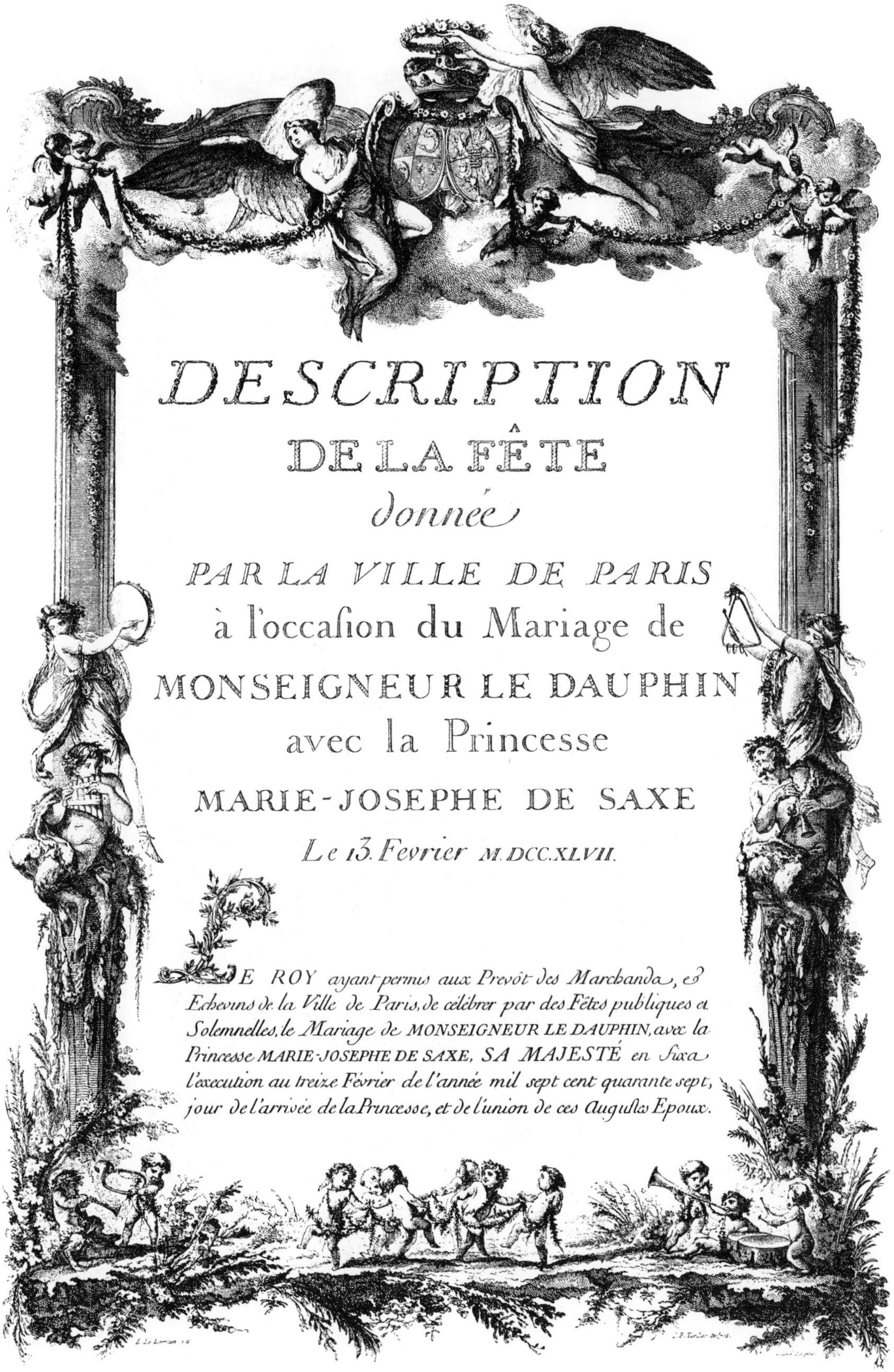

DESCRIPTION
DE LA FÊTE
donnée
PAR LA VILLE DE PARIS
à l'occasion du Mariage de
MONSEIGNEUR LE DAUPHIN
avec la Princesse
MARIE-JOSEPHE DE SAXE
Le 13. Février M.DCC.XLVII.

LE ROY ayant permis aux Prevôt des Marchands, &
Echevins de la Ville de Paris, de célébrer par des Fêtes publiques et
Solemnelles, le Mariage de MONSEIGNEUR LE DAUPHIN, avec la
Princesse MARIE-JOSEPHE DE SAXE, SA MAJESTÉ en fixa
l'exécution au treize Février de l'année mil sept cent quarante sept,
jour de l'arrivée de la Princesse, et de l'union de ces Augustes Epoux.

PLATE 120. Typical design of the mid-eighteenth century, by L. Le Lorrain.

TROISIEME LIVRE
Contenant
DES FRISES OU PANEAUX EN LONGUEUR
Inventes

PAR G.M. OPPENORT
Architecte du Roi.
Et Gravés par Huquier
Avec priv. du Roi.

PLATE 121. Engraved by Jacques Gabriel Huquier from a design by Gilles
Marie Oppenort.   Paris, about 1748.

PLATE 122. Two of Charles Eisen's designs, engraved by De Longueil.

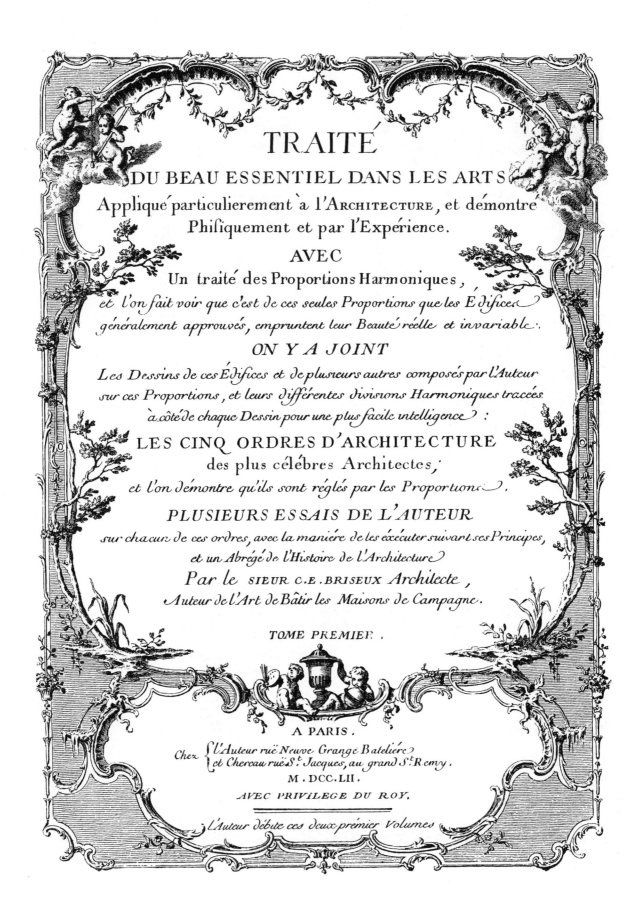

TRAITÉ

DU BEAU ESSENTIEL DANS LES ARTS

Appliqué particulierement à l'ARCHITECTURE, et démontré Phisiquement et par l'Expérience.

AVEC

Un traité des Proportions Harmoniques, et l'on fait voir que c'est de ces seules Proportions que les Édifices généralement approuvés, empruntent leur Beauté réelle et invariable.

ON Y A JOINT

Les Dessins de ces Édifices et de plusieurs autres composés par l'Auteur sur ces Proportions, et leurs différentes divisions Harmoniques tracées à côté de chaque Dessin pour une plus facile intelligence :

LES CINQ ORDRES D'ARCHITECTURE

des plus célébres Architectes, et l'on démontre qu'ils sont réglés par les Proportions.

PLUSIEURS ESSAIS DE L'AUTEUR

sur chacun de ces ordres, avec la maniére de les éxécuter suivant ses Principes, et un Abrégé de l'Histoire de l'Architecture

Par le SIEUR C.E. BRISEUX Architecte, Auteur de l'Art de Bâtir les Maisons de Campagne.

TOME PREMIER.

A PARIS.

Chez { l'Auteur ruë Neuve Grange Bateliére et Chereau ruë St. Jacques, au grand St. Remy.

M.DCC.LII.

AVEC PRIVILEGE DU ROY.

l'Auteur débite ces deux prémier Volumes

PLATE 123. Title of a treatise on architecture. Paris, 1752.

PLATE 124. Facsimile of designs by Babel; engraved by Charpentier. 1755.

AVIS AU LECTEUR DES ORDRES D'ARCHITECTURE

Le mot d'Ordre signifie dans ce grand Art un assemblage de différents corps qui étant proportionnels entre eux, et au tout, flattent la vûe, de même que l'union de plusieurs sons harmoniques procure à l'oreille une agréable sensation.

On distingue cinq ordres, savoir : le Toscan, le Dorique, l'Jonique, le Corinthien et le Composite ou Romain. Chacun de ces ordres est composé de trois parties principales, du piédestal, de la colonne et de l'entablemens qui doivent être proportionnés entre eux et à la hauteur de toutte l'ordonnance ; ces mêmes parties sont aussi subdivisées chacune en trois autres, le piédestal a sa base, son fust et son chapiteau, et l'entablement a son architrave, sa frize et sa corniche. J'ai pensé qu'il étoit à propos pour en doner d'abord une idée d'en dessiner les figures, et donner à entendre ce que c'est que module qui n'est autre chose qu'une mesure de la longueur du semi-diamètre de la colonne que vous voulez construire, sans pourtant y marquer les mesures, parce qu'en cecy mon desseu n'est autre que de représenter tous d'un coûp l'effet d'une règle générale dont je ferai dans la suite l'application à chaque ordre en particulier.

PLATE 125. A facsimile of a title drawn and engraved by Babel. 1755.

PLATE 126. Facsimiles of decorative pieces drawn by Babel. 1755.

VUË DU BATIMENT
DE LA GALERIE ROYALE DE DRESDE.

A. Elevation de la Façade. B. Elevation de la Façade laterale.

PLATE 127. Title by Charles Eisen; engraved by Noël Le Mire. 1756.

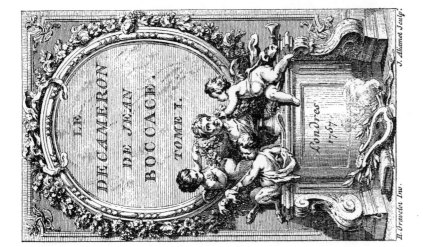

PLATE 128. Designs by the famous Hubert François Gravelot. 1757–1761.

PLATE 129. Facsimile drawings from Bachelier's flowers. Paris, 1762.

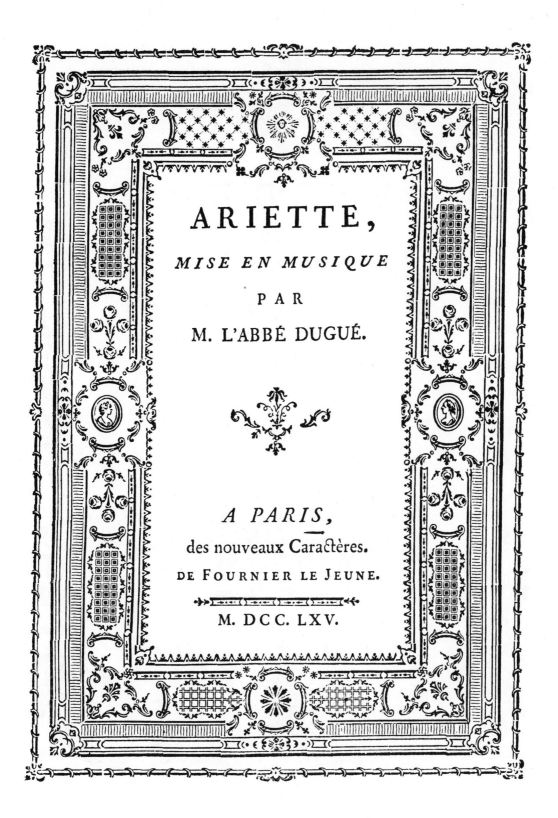

ARIETTE,

MISE EN MUSIQUE

PAR

M. L'ABBÉ DUGUÉ.

A PARIS,

des nouveaux Caractères.

DE FOURNIER LE JEUNE.

M. DCC. LXV.

PLATE 130. Typographic title by Fournier le jeune.   Paris, 1765.

PLATE 131. A German title in the rococo manner. 1767.

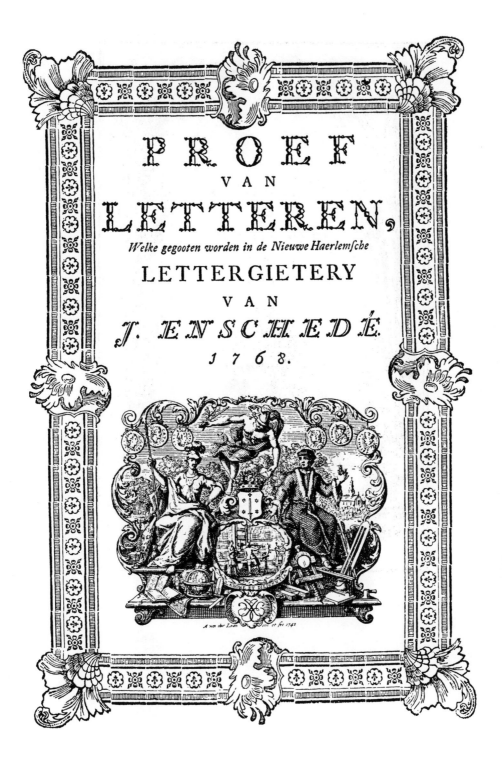

PLATE 132. The use of printers' flowers by Enschedé. 1768.

ZULMÉNIE
ET
VOLSIDOR
CONTE
TOM. II.

C. P. Marillier inv. 1776.

D. Née Sculp

PLATE 133. Title design by Clément Pierre Marillier, draftsman and etcher.
1776.

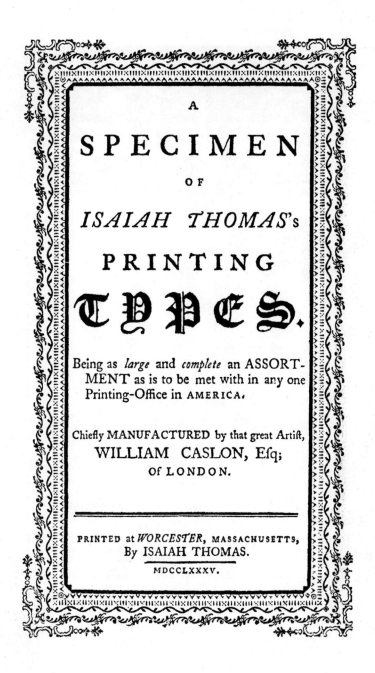

A

SPECIMEN

OF

ISAIAH THOMAS's

PRINTING

𝔗𝔶𝔭𝔢𝔰.

Being as *large* and *complete* an ASSORT-
MENT as is to be met with in any one
Printing-Office in AMERICA.

Chiefly MANUFACTURED by that great Artiſt,
WILLIAM CASLON, Eſq;
Of LONDON.

PRINTED at *WORCESTER*, MASSACHUSETTS,
By ISAIAH THOMAS.
MDCCLXXXV.

PLATE 134. Printers' flowers as used by Isaiah Thomas.   Worcester,
Massachusetts, 1785.

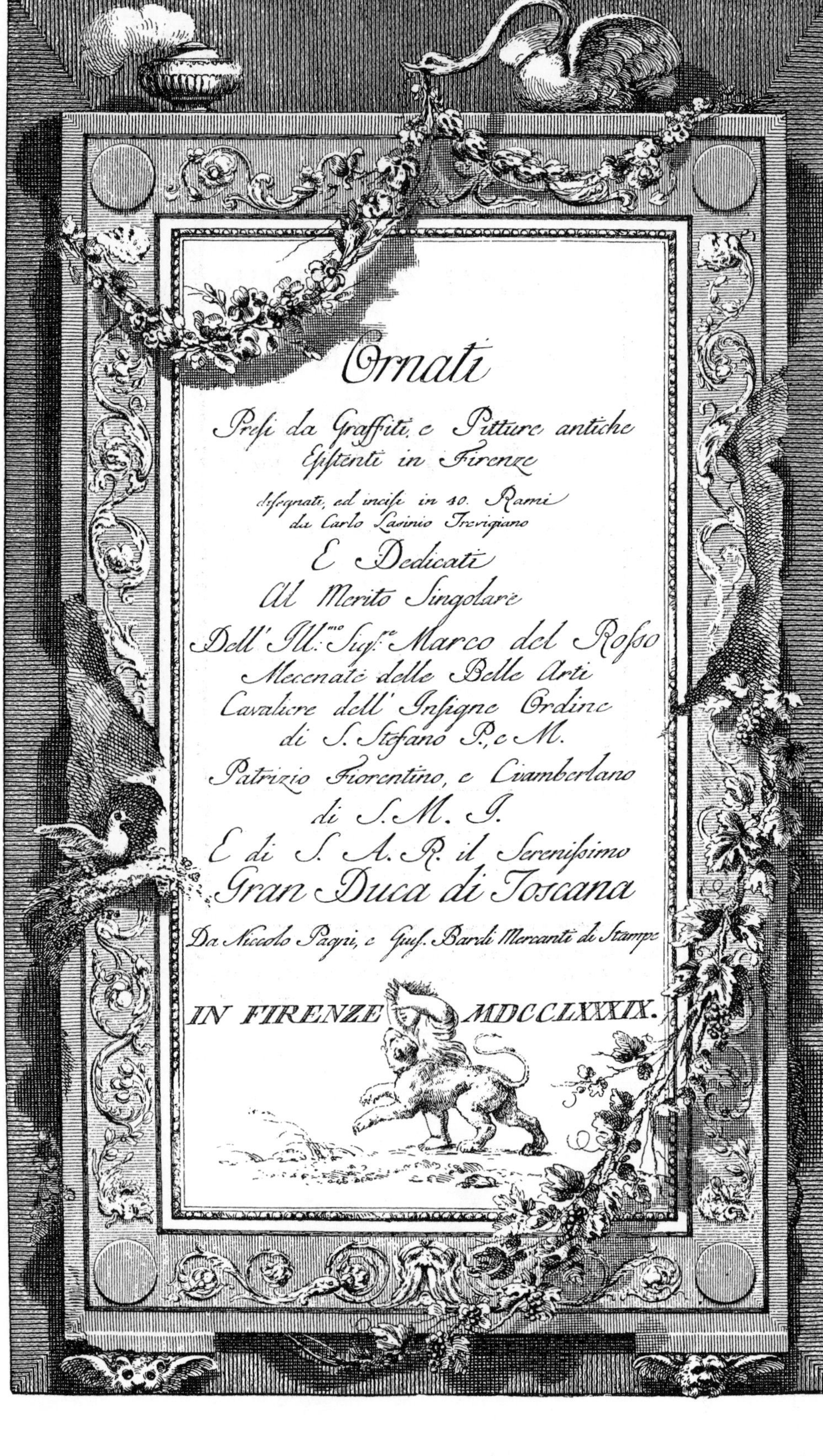

PLATE 135. An Italian title by Carlo Lasinio. Florence, 1789.

C.P. Marillier, Del.　　　　　　　　　　　　　　　　　　　　　　　N. Ponce, Sculp.

LOUIS HECTOR DUC DE VILLARS,

Pair et Maréchal de France, Ministre d'État, Mar.ᶜʰ Gén.ᵃˡ des Camps et Armées du Roi, Grand d'Espagne &c. Né à Moulins en 1651, mort à Turin le 17 Juin 1734.

Le jeune Villars, d'abord Aide de Camp du M.ᵃˡ de Bellefonds son parent, se signala dans plusieurs occasions, notament au passage du Rhin, et au Siege de Mastricht. La valeur qu'il déploya à la Bat.ᵉ de Senef, où il fut blessé, lui valut un Régi.ᵐᵗ de Caval.ᵉ Honoré du grade de M.ᵃˡ de Camp, il contribua au succès de la journée de Leuse, et participa l'An.ᵉᵉ suivante au gain de la Bat.ᵉ de Phorteen. La Paix ayant été conclue à Ryswich, il passa à Vienne en qualité d'Amba.ʳ Extra.ʳᵉ De la cet Off.ᵉʳ Gén.ᵃˡ fut envoyé en Italie à la mort du Roi d'Esp.ⁿᵉ et il y signala son arrivée par la déf.ᵗᵉ d'un Corps de Troupes qui projettoit de l'enlever. Passant ensuite en Allé.ᵐⁿᵉ il traverse le Rhin à la vue des Enne.ᵐⁱˢ s'empare de Neubourg, remporte une viet.ᵉ sur le Pr.ᶜᵉ de Bade à Fridlinghen, et l'An.ᵉᵉ d'après bat complᵗ des enn.ˢ à Hoch.ᵗˡᵗ. Villars ayant été appelé en Languedoc pour soumettre les Vaudois que la persécution de Louis XIV avoit fait soulever, il parvint à rétablir le calme dans cette Prov.ⁿᵉ Étant repassé en Allem.ᵉ en 1707, pour s'opposer aux succès de Marleboroug, il vainquit les

alliés à Stolhoffen. Le Duc de Savoye ayant pénétré en Dauphiné l'Année suivante, Villars fit avorter tous les desseins de ce Prince. Rappelé en Flandre pour y arrêter les progrès de l'Armée ennemie, il la combatit à Malplaquet, et fut dangereusᵗ blessé dans cette jour.ᵉᵉ Louis XIV humilié de toute part, Landrecies assiégé par Eugène, il ne reste plus d'espoir à la France que dans le courage et l'habileté de Villars : son espéranᶜᵉ n'est pas vaine ; ce Héros tombe à l'improviste sur Dénain, où une partie de l'Armée des alliés étoit retranchée, il la disperse, s'empare de cette Place, du Fort de Scarpe, de Marchiennes, de Douay, du Quénoy et de Bouchain, et par suite de Landau et de Fribourg. Alors les ennemis consternés consentent enfin à la Paix, que le Vainqueur signa à Rastadt en 1713. Ayant accepté le Comm.ᵗ de l'Armée d'Italie en 1733, la mort qui le surprit à Turin mit un terme à ses glo.ʳᵉˢ exploits. Le Comˢ.ᵗᵉ de Dénain sera à jamais mém.ᵉ dans l'Hisᵗ. L'audace de Villars à la Gueᵉ sa présompⁿᵉ à la Cour, et son amour pour l'argent sont quelques légᵉʳ taches à sa mémoire, que ses talens émin.ˢ et ses importᵗ services font facileᵗ oublier.

A. P. D. R.

A Paris chez l'Auteur
Cloitre extérieur du Val-de-Grâce
N.º 238.

PLATE 136. Another design by Clément Pierre Marillier. 1790.

HOLY BIBLE

Ornamented with Engravings

By

JAMES FITTLER

From

Celebrated Pictures

By

OLD MASTERS

The Letter Preſs,

By Thomas Bensley

LONDON, Publiſhed by R. Bowyer, Historic Gallery, Pall Mall, & J. Fittler, Nº 62, Upper Charlotte Street. 1795.

Tomkins Scr. Vincent Scu.

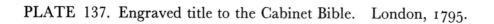

PLATE 137. Engraved title to the Cabinet Bible. London, 1795.

III. The Nineteenth Century and Beyond

III. The Nineteenth Century and Beyond

Style, in the sense in which it had evolved through all previous time, came to an end with the final triumph of the industrial revolution. The complete displacement of the handicraftsman brought to an end the entire process of passing craft methods, aesthetic viewpoints, and master's techniques from generation to generation in such a way that styles grew and changed organically within societies. Of course, the change that occurred should not be stated as simply as that; but for our purposes it may be said that the overall aspect of the decorative arts was strongly influenced by the factors of the growing industrial production and the new power groups in society.

There was, too, a completely new interest in cultures other than the Greek and Roman as sources for decoration and ornament. Commerce was opening avenues into the most remote areas of the world; the artists and designers of the nineteenth century were inspired by and copied all sorts of decorative material, indiscriminately and with little knowledge or feeling about truly creative work methods. This mere copying or imitating of all kinds of earlier work seemed to be the only way in which it was possible to cope with the massive demands of the new production and the wants of a dislocated society. The result was a general decline in the intrinsic quality of all the arts. Much of the output was expertly done, technically quite good; but certainly it lacked greatness from the point of view of true style.

The titles in this third section lead through many confusing byways to the point in our own century at which the decorative title was once more abandoned. All through the nineteenth century there were changes in the techniques of reproducing the illustrations and decorative material in books; Aloys Senefelder's title (138), for example, is evidence of his new reproduction process, lithography.

A study of the William Pickering titles produced in the 1840's (143, 144, 145, 148, 157, 158) will reveal his rather determined attempt to produce books in the manner of Aldus Manutius; new methods and machinery were used to print these books, which have the format and ornament of the sixteenth and seventeenth centuries rather than the style of Aldus. The Whittinghams, who printed for Pickering, did an excellent job; the engravers who were employed were capable technical craftsmen; but this whole effort was revivalistic, archaic—it did not really spring from the work itself nor from any expressive depth in the workers involved.

Seven borders from *Beauties of the Opera and Ballet* (149, 150, 151, 152, 153, 154, 155), probably printed in 1844, have been included although they are not strictly titles. As stock borders they could have been used for titles and they do reflect accurately the use of ornament in books of the period. The range is from the grassy, leafy, sweet, and sentimental to rather severe repeat patterns taken from tiles, lace, and other historic designs.

These glimpses into two areas of book-design activity will suffice for the great mass of book publishing in Europe and the United States. Most of this production was rather similar to these examples, but in general not as good. In the second half of the nineteenth century there was a decline from even this fair standard of technical quality and honest production. Into this welter of non-creative design came, finally, the powerful strivings of William Morris and his group. They made a frontal assault on the tawdry and shoddy in man's environment: his home, furniture, fabrics, crockery, utensils, and his books. We are only concerned with the last-named, and two of Morris's titles (168, 169) have been reproduced to note the rebirth of quality and vitality in design. Morris was, of course, influenced by the great books of the incunabula period; but, essentially, he expressed himself and his time. It is instantly apparent that there is a surge of genuine creative power in these pages.

There was a certain something in the air of all Europe, and even of the United States, at the turn of the century. Groups in England, France, Germany, Austria, Holland, and Belgium began to work in new ways. Typical of this concern with the course of development in all the arts, the new style, *Jugendstil* or *art nouveau*, made itself manifest in the art of the book. A designer such as Otto Eckmann (174) may be said to typify the whole movement. Again, there is the impression of power and a new approach; there is a perception of organic growth, based on plant forms, but actually verging on non-objective ornament. There were definite Morris and *Jugendstil* influences in the United States; Will Bradley's work (175, 176) shows this. However, the conservative elements in the decorative arts continued reproducing historic designs until quite recently.

European functional typography finally dispensed with the use of ornament almost entirely. The only ornament allowed in the severe typography of the 1930's was the line in all its varying weights, or other typographic units that were used purely for their impact value or direction. American book design was much affected by these successive influences from abroad; although William Dwiggins developed a personal style of book decoration, ornament has disappeared from the book and the title-page.

The search for style goes on; all the arts have become modish, and fashions change from year to year if not from season to season. Whether the use of the decorative title will return is problematical; but it would seem that man may tire of the sterile, the inhuman, and the unattractive, and in some way begin to ornament his creations and his surroundings once more.

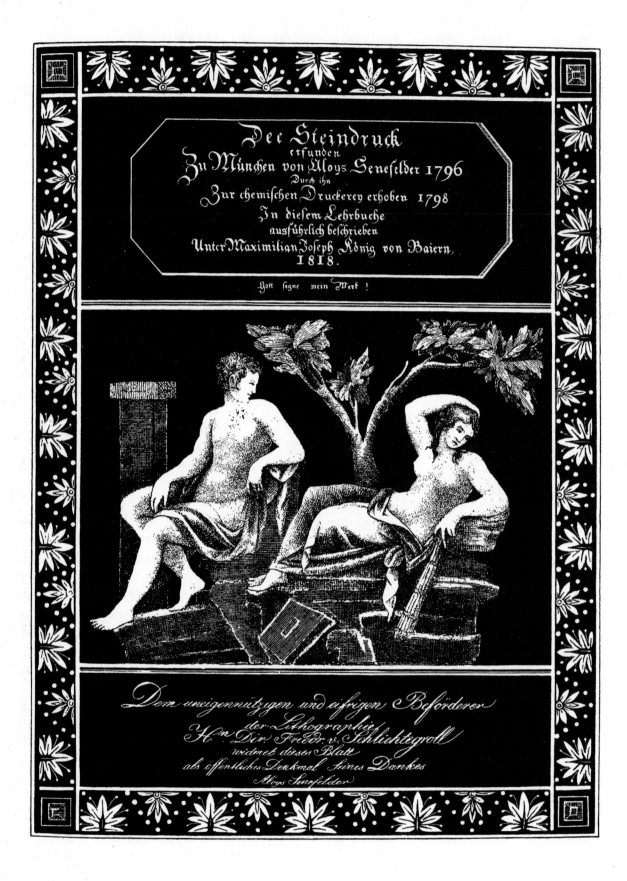

PLATE 138. A title design by Aloys Senefelder, discoverer of lithography.
1818.

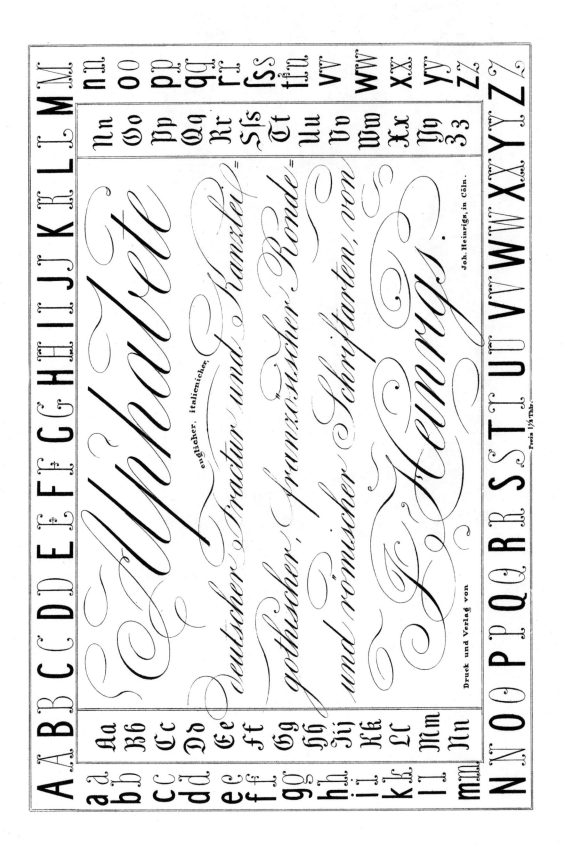

PLATE 139. The title to Johann Heinrig's writing book. Cologne, 1834.

PLATE 140. From the first illustrated edition of this book. Paris, 1838.

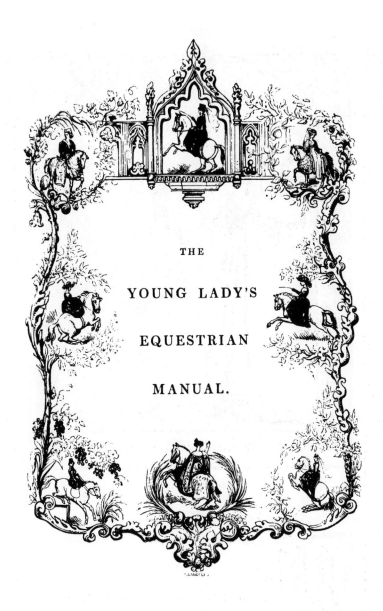

THE

YOUNG LADY'S

EQUESTRIAN

MANUAL.

PLATE 141. The rococo lived on in such titles as this.   London, 1838.

Wie Siegfried Chriemhilden zuerst ersah.

Fünftes Abenteuer.

Man sah nun alle Tage hin nach dem Rheine reiten:
Sie kamen zu dem Feste vom Nahen und vom Weiten;
Und die zu Lieb dem Könige den Weg ins Land genommen,
Die haben zur Genüge Rosse und Kleider bekommen.

PLATE 142. Romanticism in the German area. Design by Eduard Bendemann, 1840.

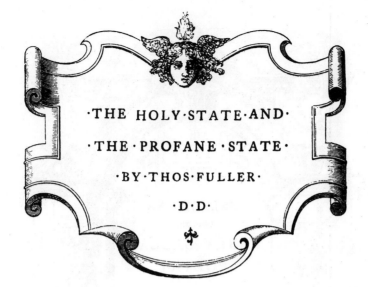

·THE·HOLY·STATE·AND·

·THE·PROFANE·STATE·

·BY·THOS·FULLER·

·D·D·

LONDON

WILLIAM PICKERING

1840

PLATE 143. A title used by William Pickering, related to seventeenth-century scrolls; the mark derived from Aldus Manutius.   London, 1840.

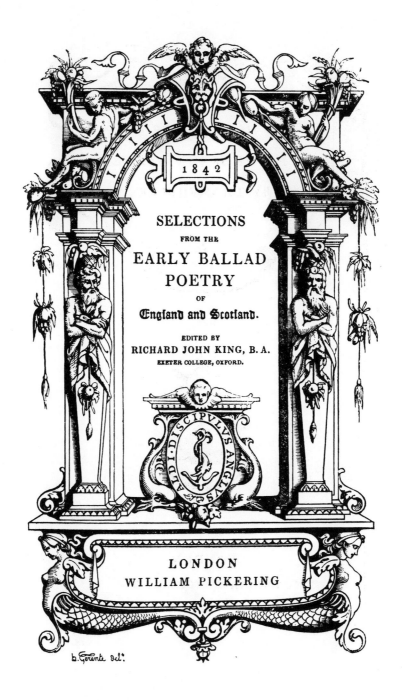

SELECTIONS

FROM THE

EARLY BALLAD
POETRY

OF

𝔈𝔫𝔤𝔩𝔞𝔫𝔡 𝔞𝔫𝔡 𝔖𝔠𝔬𝔱𝔩𝔞𝔫𝔡.

EDITED BY

RICHARD JOHN KING, B.A.
EXETER COLLEGE, OXFORD.

LONDON
WILLIAM PICKERING

PLATE 144. Another Pickering title, based on various sixteenth-century
designs. London, 1842.

The·vision·and·the·creed·of
Piers·Ploughman
newly·imprinted

London·William·Pickering
M dccc xxxxij

PLATE 145. A variant of the Pickering device used with head- and foot-pieces.
London, 1842.

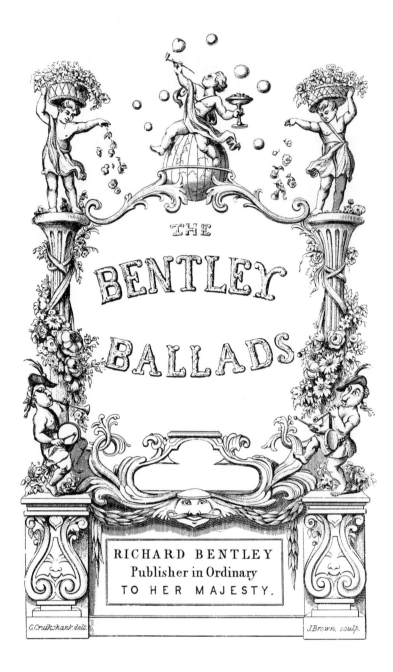

THE

BENTLEY

BALLADS

RICHARD BENTLEY
Publisher in Ordinary
TO HER MAJESTY.

G.Cruikshank.delt.

J.Brown. sculp.

PLATE 146. A George Cruikshank title, produced for the famous publisher, Bentley.

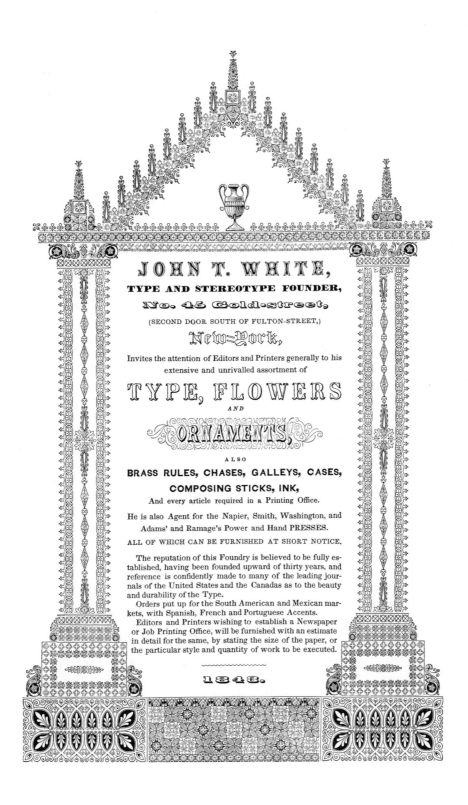

PLATE 147. A typographic title for a type founder's specimen book.   New York.

PLATE 148. An elaborate title for Pickering's *The Book of Common Prayer*.   London.

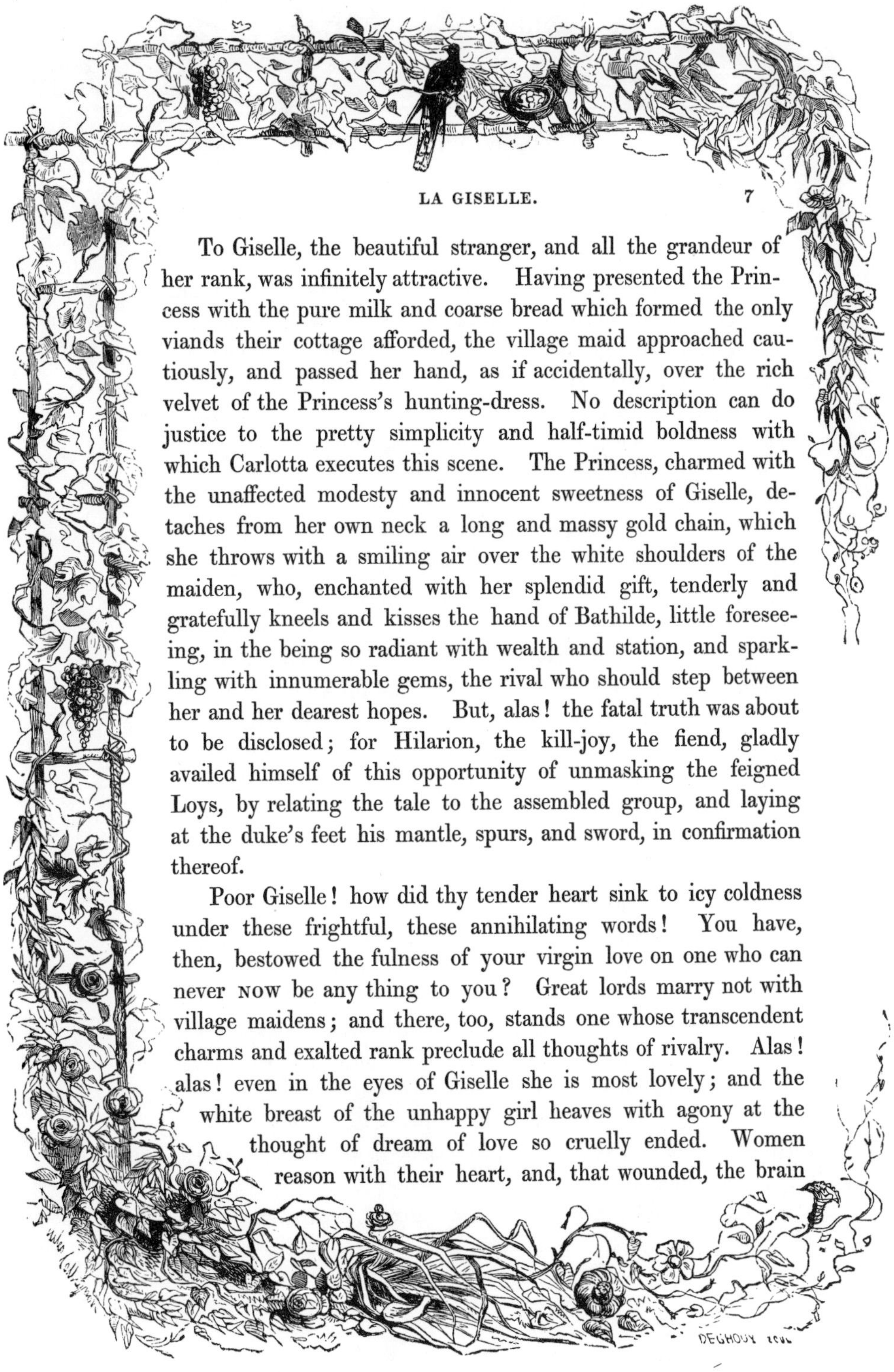

To Giselle, the beautiful stranger, and all the grandeur of her rank, was infinitely attractive. Having presented the Princess with the pure milk and coarse bread which formed the only viands their cottage afforded, the village maid approached cautiously, and passed her hand, as if accidentally, over the rich velvet of the Princess's hunting-dress. No description can do justice to the pretty simplicity and half-timid boldness with which Carlotta executes this scene. The Princess, charmed with the unaffected modesty and innocent sweetness of Giselle, detaches from her own neck a long and massy gold chain, which she throws with a smiling air over the white shoulders of the maiden, who, enchanted with her splendid gift, tenderly and gratefully kneels and kisses the hand of Bathilde, little foreseeing, in the being so radiant with wealth and station, and sparkling with innumerable gems, the rival who should step between her and her dearest hopes. But, alas! the fatal truth was about to be disclosed; for Hilarion, the kill-joy, the fiend, gladly availed himself of this opportunity of unmasking the feigned Loys, by relating the tale to the assembled group, and laying at the duke's feet his mantle, spurs, and sword, in confirmation thereof.

Poor Giselle! how did thy tender heart sink to icy coldness under these frightful, these annihilating words! You have, then, bestowed the fulness of your virgin love on one who can never NOW be any thing to you? Great lords marry not with village maidens; and there, too, stands one whose transcendent charms and exalted rank preclude all thoughts of rivalry. Alas! alas! even in the eyes of Giselle she is most lovely; and the white breast of the unhappy girl heaves with agony at the thought of dream of love so cruelly ended. Women reason with their heart, and, that wounded, the brain

PLATE 149. The first of seven pages from *Beauties of the Opera and Ballet.* Probably 1844.

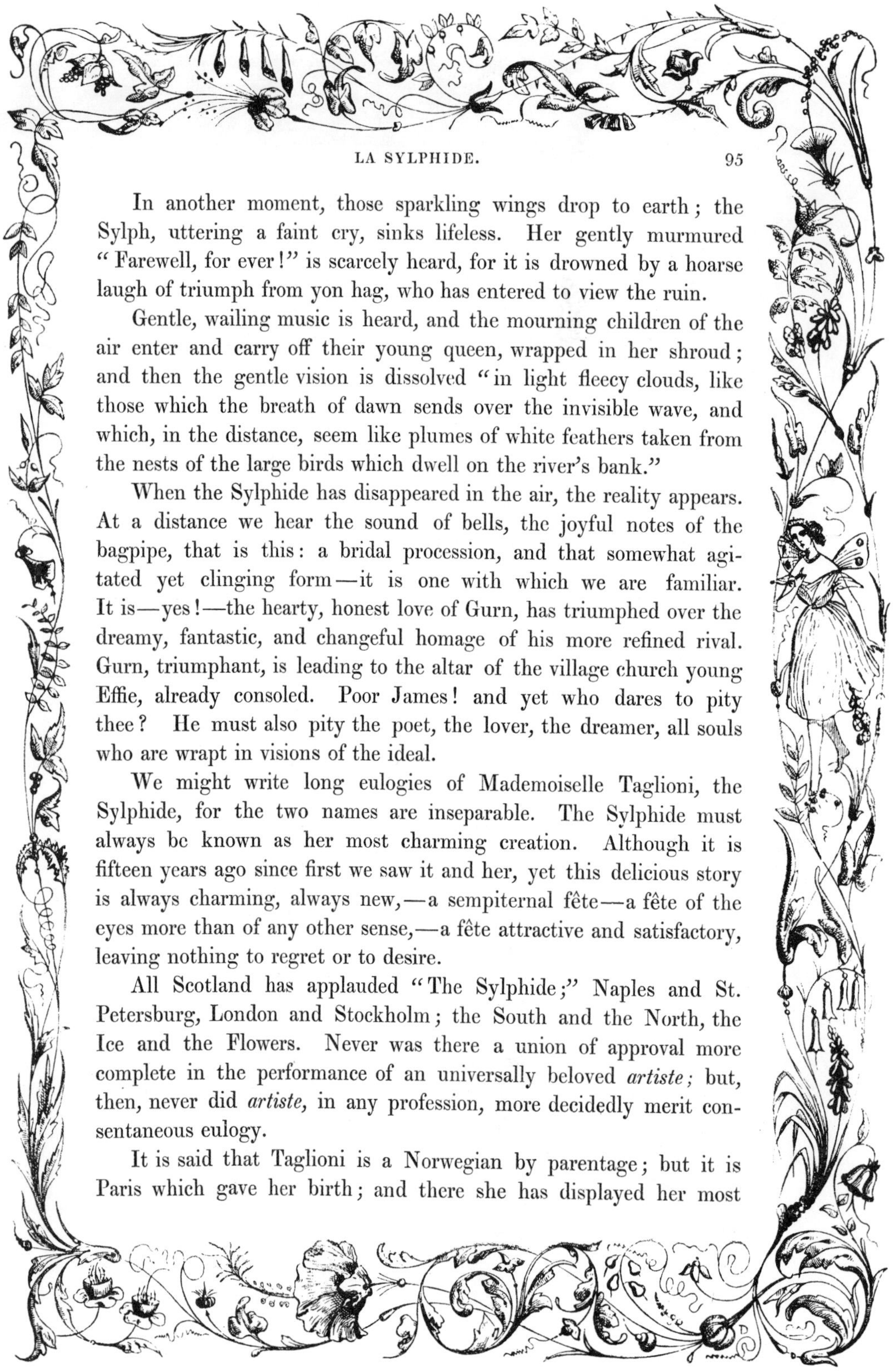

In another moment, those sparkling wings drop to earth ; the Sylph, uttering a faint cry, sinks lifeless. Her gently murmured "Farewell, for ever!" is scarcely heard, for it is drowned by a hoarse laugh of triumph from yon hag, who has entered to view the ruin.

Gentle, wailing music is heard, and the mourning children of the air enter and carry off their young queen, wrapped in her shroud ; and then the gentle vision is dissolved "in light fleecy clouds, like those which the breath of dawn sends over the invisible wave, and which, in the distance, seem like plumes of white feathers taken from the nests of the large birds which dwell on the river's bank."

When the Sylphide has disappeared in the air, the reality appears. At a distance we hear the sound of bells, the joyful notes of the bagpipe, that is this : a bridal procession, and that somewhat agitated yet clinging form—it is one with which we are familiar. It is—yes!—the hearty, honest love of Gurn, has triumphed over the dreamy, fantastic, and changeful homage of his more refined rival. Gurn, triumphant, is leading to the altar of the village church young Effie, already consoled. Poor James! and yet who dares to pity thee? He must also pity the poet, the lover, the dreamer, all souls who are wrapt in visions of the ideal.

We might write long eulogies of Mademoiselle Taglioni, the Sylphide, for the two names are inseparable. The Sylphide must always be known as her most charming creation. Although it is fifteen years ago since first we saw it and her, yet this delicious story is always charming, always new,—a sempiternal fête—a fête of the eyes more than of any other sense,—a fête attractive and satisfactory, leaving nothing to regret or to desire.

All Scotland has applauded "The Sylphide;" Naples and St. Petersburg, London and Stockholm; the South and the North, the Ice and the Flowers. Never was there a union of approval more complete in the performance of an universally beloved *artiste*; but, then, never did *artiste*, in any profession, more decidedly merit consentaneous eulogy.

It is said that Taglioni is a Norwegian by parentage; but it is Paris which gave her birth; and there she has displayed her most

PLATE 150. This border was drawn to relate to the ballet, *La Sylphide*.

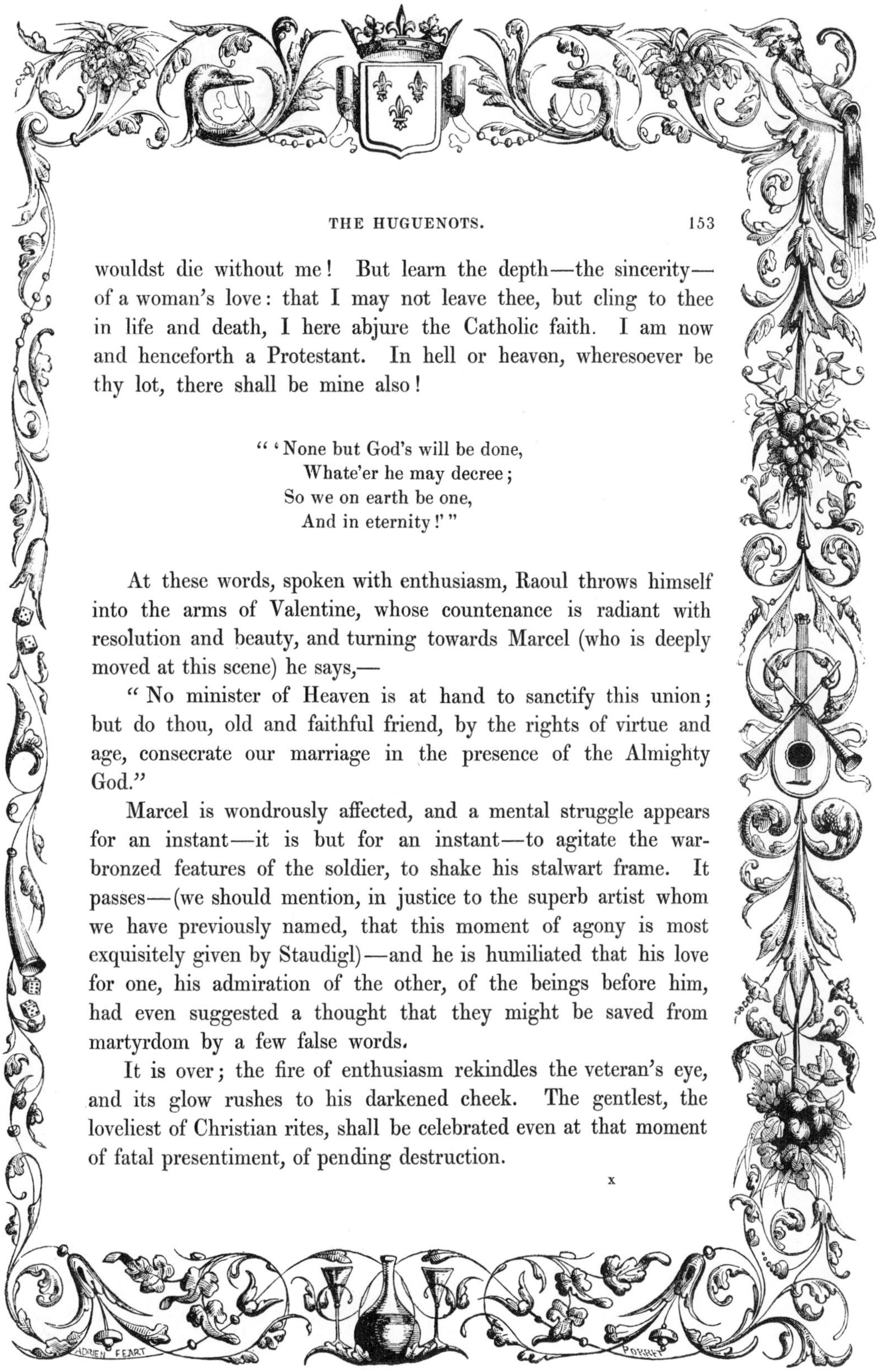

wouldst die without me! But learn the depth—the sincerity—
of a woman's love: that I may not leave thee, but cling to thee
in life and death, I here abjure the Catholic faith. I am now
and henceforth a Protestant. In hell or heaven, wheresoever be
thy lot, there shall be mine also!

> " ' None but God's will be done,
>   Whate'er he may decree;
>   So we on earth be one,
>   And in eternity!' "

At these words, spoken with enthusiasm, Raoul throws himself
into the arms of Valentine, whose countenance is radiant with
resolution and beauty, and turning towards Marcel (who is deeply
moved at this scene) he says,—

"No minister of Heaven is at hand to sanctify this union;
but do thou, old and faithful friend, by the rights of virtue and
age, consecrate our marriage in the presence of the Almighty
God."

Marcel is wondrously affected, and a mental struggle appears
for an instant—it is but for an instant—to agitate the war-
bronzed features of the soldier, to shake his stalwart frame. It
passes—(we should mention, in justice to the superb artist whom
we have previously named, that this moment of agony is most
exquisitely given by Staudigl)—and he is humiliated that his love
for one, his admiration of the other, of the beings before him,
had even suggested a thought that they might be saved from
martyrdom by a few false words.

It is over; the fire of enthusiasm rekindles the veteran's eye,
and its glow rushes to his darkened cheek. The gentlest, the
loveliest of Christian rites, shall be celebrated even at that moment
of fatal presentiment, of pending destruction.

x

PLATE 151. Here the border is related to the opera, *The Huguenots.*

listens eagerly. He hopes that the sight of the rack, or, at most, its first pang, will produce the effect he sighs for. But no messenger returns—still no summons. He paces the dungeon, and shudders at the deed which is now being done under his orders.

Ha! that yell of inexpressible anguish rings through the prison—will ring through the brain of the Cardinal till his dying day. Is that a groan which follows, or is it but the echo of his own remorseful murmur?

There is no further sound.

A messenger at last—his step is hasty—the Cardinal springs to meet him.

" Will he confess?"

" Your Eminence, no!"

" What!—what means have been tried?"

" All, your Eminence; and if he is to survive for the scaffold——"

" Take him thither."

And the baffled father leaves the prison—he will yet try one more effort upon the scene of death.

The last scene! We have the great square of Constance, crowded with spectators, and lined with soldiery. In the foreground is the platform, with the dreadful caldron, under which the flames still glow, though the scalding liquid within is tossing and hissing in fiery waves. A short flight of steps has been placed beside it, to enable the executioners to carry up their victim. The Cardinal appears, attended, and takes his place on the right, and the various ministers of the law are already present.

And now the doomed maiden is seen to mount the scaffold; her head droops upon her bosom, and her long raven tresses fall dishevelled over her beautiful shoulders. Yet her tread is firm, her eye steady—love has converted the martyr into the heroine.

She looks around for her father, but sees him not. Can they have murdered him, without allowing her one last embrace? She rushes to the Cardinal's feet.

PLATE 152. This is a design somewhat based on the opera, *The Jewess.*

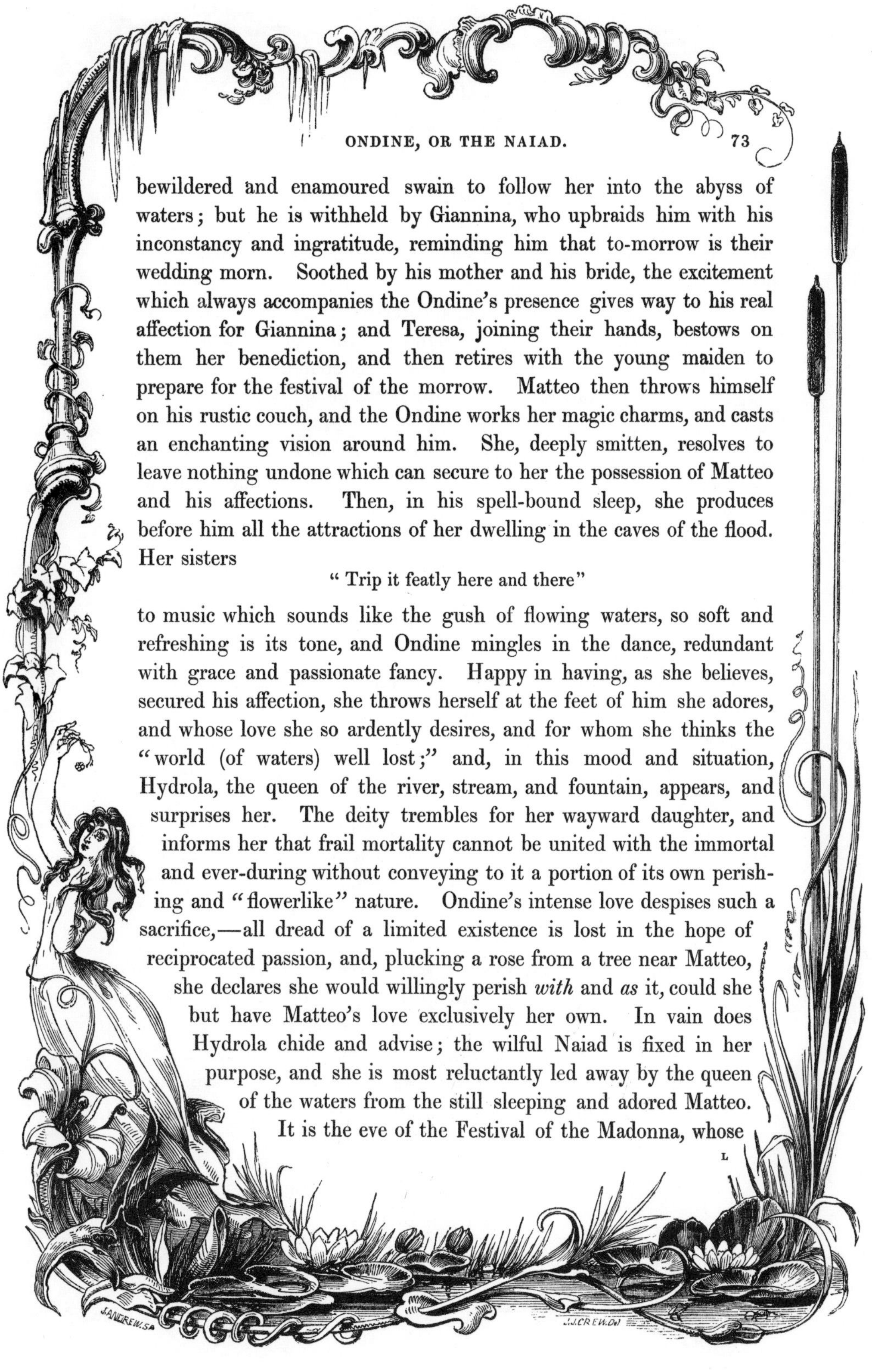

bewildered and enamoured swain to follow her into the abyss of waters; but he is withheld by Giannina, who upbraids him with his inconstancy and ingratitude, reminding him that to-morrow is their wedding morn. Soothed by his mother and his bride, the excitement which always accompanies the Ondine's presence gives way to his real affection for Giannina; and Teresa, joining their hands, bestows on them her benediction, and then retires with the young maiden to prepare for the festival of the morrow. Matteo then throws himself on his rustic couch, and the Ondine works her magic charms, and casts an enchanting vision around him. She, deeply smitten, resolves to leave nothing undone which can secure to her the possession of Matteo and his affections. Then, in his spell-bound sleep, she produces before him all the attractions of her dwelling in the caves of the flood. Her sisters

"Trip it featly here and there"

to music which sounds like the gush of flowing waters, so soft and refreshing is its tone, and Ondine mingles in the dance, redundant with grace and passionate fancy. Happy in having, as she believes, secured his affection, she throws herself at the feet of him she adores, and whose love she so ardently desires, and for whom she thinks the "world (of waters) well lost;" and, in this mood and situation, Hydrola, the queen of the river, stream, and fountain, appears, and surprises her. The deity trembles for her wayward daughter, and informs her that frail mortality cannot be united with the immortal and ever-during without conveying to it a portion of its own perishing and "flowerlike" nature. Ondine's intense love despises such a sacrifice,—all dread of a limited existence is lost in the hope of reciprocated passion, and, plucking a rose from a tree near Matteo, she declares she would willingly perish *with* and *as* it, could she but have Matteo's love exclusively her own. In vain does Hydrola chide and advise; the wilful Naiad is fixed in her purpose, and she is most reluctantly led away by the queen of the waters from the still sleeping and adored Matteo.

It is the eve of the Festival of the Madonna, whose

L

PLATE 153. A very definite relation to the theme of the ballet, *Ondine*.

"Arise, priest—arise! What! kneeling to a Jew?"

And, with a hollow laugh, he turns his back upon the Cardinal, who, in the deepest dejection, retires, unable to gain from Eleazar the secret, the possession of which would, he dreams, render happy the remainder of his life.

Ha! a thought has helped him, and revived his hopes. The obstinate Jew, accursed alike of God and man, refuses to the agonies of a father the knowledge where his own, his only child, is to be found. What mercy does so merciless a wretch deserve at that father's hands? Tears, prayers, have failed to extort the secret. Will the Jew yield it to the *rack?*

There is but little time to lose, for the great bell of the Cathedral is already sounding the knell of the Hebrews. Speedily the Cardinal re-appears, with stern determination in his looks.

"Eleazar!"

"Again, priest? May not the Jew's last minutes be spent in communion with his God?"

"Thy God, Jew! Deserve his mercy by one—one act of humanity. Where is my child?"

"Have I not sworn to withhold the secret? Begone, nor think I will add perjury to my sins in my dying hour."

"That hour shall be more bitter than thy wildest fears can imagine. Enter!" And, in answer to the raised voice of the Cardinal, six masked forms appear.

"These, Jew, are the torturers. The agonies which they can crowd into one half hour are only known to themselves and to the wretches who have shrieked their lives out within these walls. Disclose thy secret, or learn theirs."

"Christian priest—never!"

"Drag him to the torture-vault," exclaims the Cardinal, in the extreme of rage; "and, while he has bone to crush or joint to wrench, use all your engines upon him. I—I will not be present at the work; but I will remain here. The instant he consents to confess, summon me."

Pale, but firm, Eleazar is hurried from the presence of the Cardinal. De Brogni, half repenting, yet burning to hear tidings of his child,

PLATE 154. A curiously grotesque border for the opera, *The Jewess.*

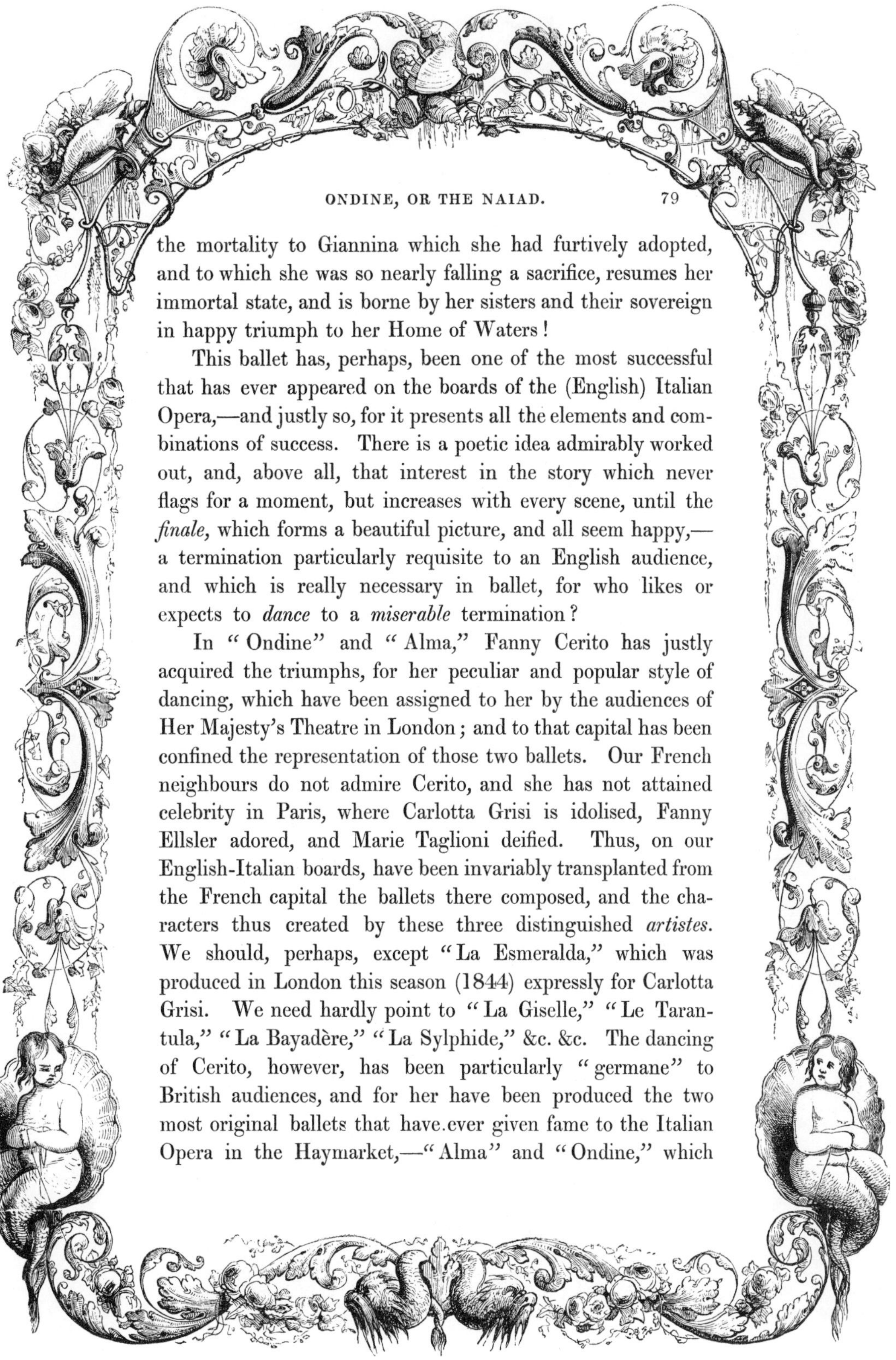

the mortality to Giannina which she had furtively adopted, and to which she was so nearly falling a sacrifice, resumes her immortal state, and is borne by her sisters and their sovereign in happy triumph to her Home of Waters!

This ballet has, perhaps, been one of the most successful that has ever appeared on the boards of the (English) Italian Opera,—and justly so, for it presents all the elements and combinations of success. There is a poetic idea admirably worked out, and, above all, that interest in the story which never flags for a moment, but increases with every scene, until the *finale*, which forms a beautiful picture, and all seem happy,— a termination particularly requisite to an English audience, and which is really necessary in ballet, for who likes or expects to *dance* to a *miserable* termination?

In "Ondine" and "Alma," Fanny Cerito has justly acquired the triumphs, for her peculiar and popular style of dancing, which have been assigned to her by the audiences of Her Majesty's Theatre in London; and to that capital has been confined the representation of those two ballets. Our French neighbours do not admire Cerito, and she has not attained celebrity in Paris, where Carlotta Grisi is idolised, Fanny Ellsler adored, and Marie Taglioni deified. Thus, on our English-Italian boards, have been invariably transplanted from the French capital the ballets there composed, and the characters thus created by these three distinguished *artistes*. We should, perhaps, except "La Esmeralda," which was produced in London this season (1844) expressly for Carlotta Grisi. We need hardly point to "La Giselle," "Le Tarantula," "La Bayadère," "La Sylphide," &c. &c. The dancing of Cerito, however, has been particularly "germane" to British audiences, and for her have been produced the two most original ballets that have ever given fame to the Italian Opera in the Haymarket,—"Alma" and "Ondine," which

PLATE 155. The last of the pages from *Beauties of the Opera and Ballet*.

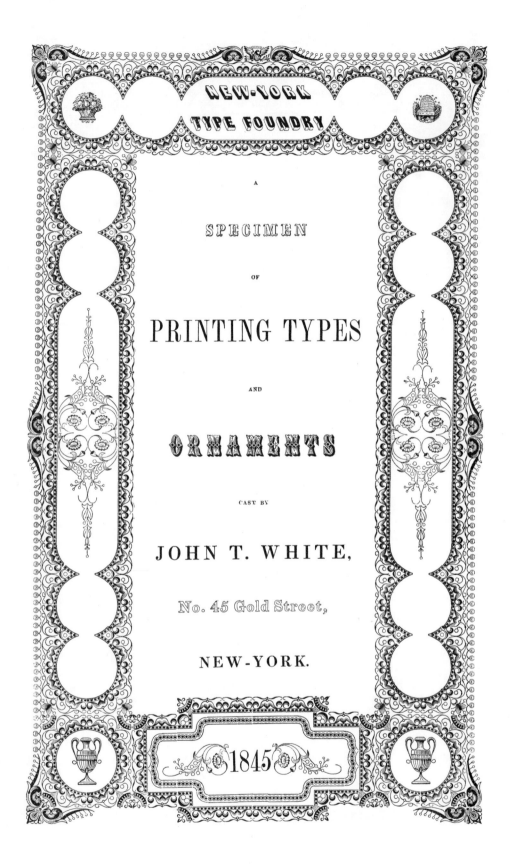

PLATE 156. The title to the John T. White specimen book of 1845.

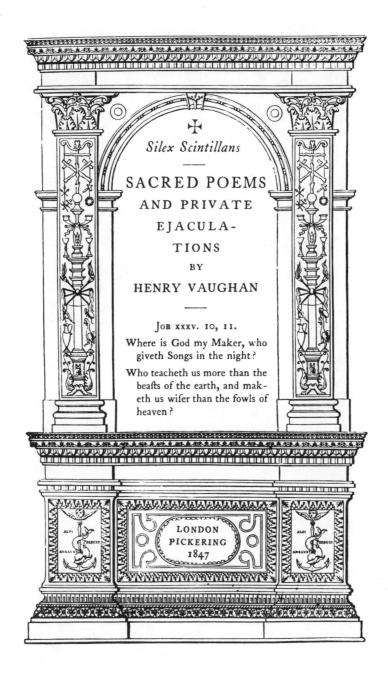

PLATE 157. The basis for this Pickering design is to be found in earlier titles.

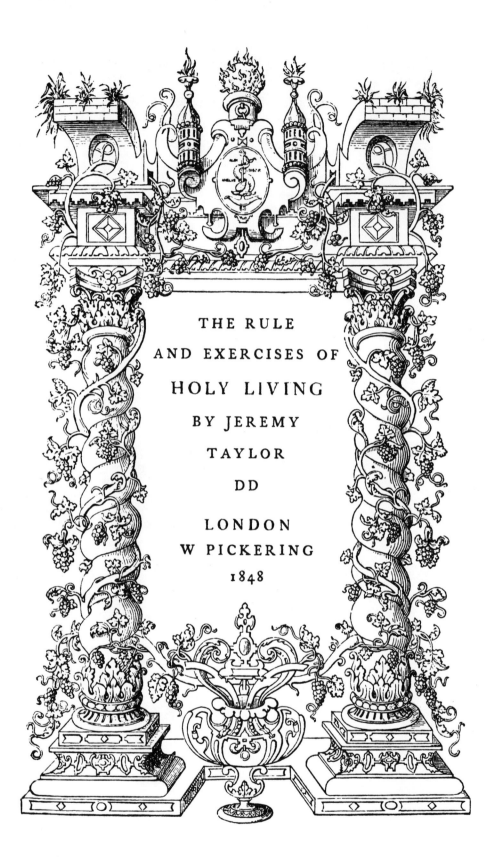

THE RULE
AND EXERCISES OF
HOLY LIVING
BY JEREMY
TAYLOR
DD

LONDON
W PICKERING
1848

PLATE 158. A Pickering title based on designs of the sixteenth and seventeenth centuries. 1848.

PLATE 159. Headings of a magazine dealing with ornament and decoration.

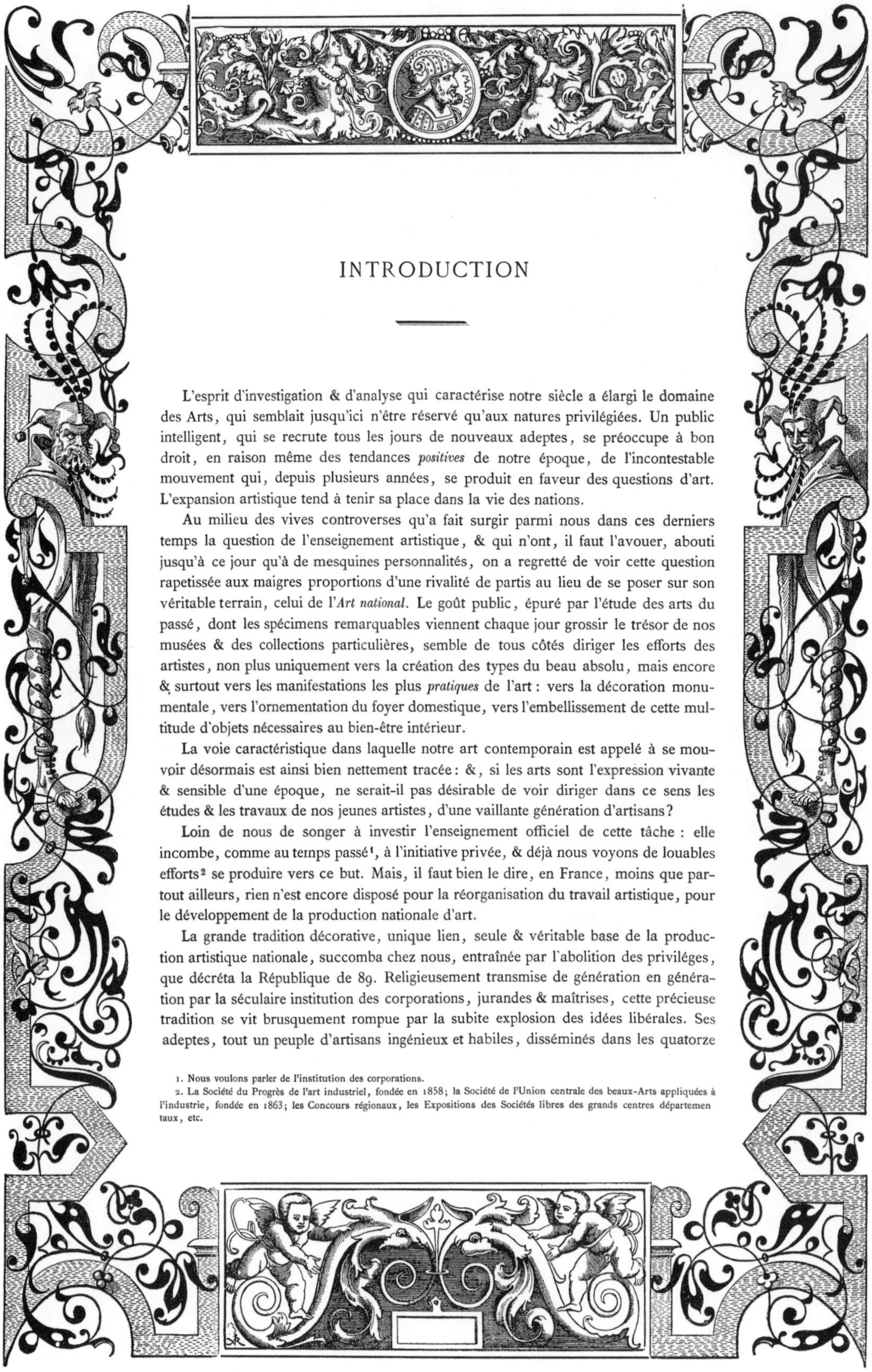

INTRODUCTION

L'esprit d'investigation & d'analyse qui caractérise notre siècle a élargi le domaine des Arts, qui semblait jusqu'ici n'être réservé qu'aux natures privilégiées. Un public intelligent, qui se recrute tous les jours de nouveaux adeptes, se préoccupe à bon droit, en raison même des tendances *positives* de notre époque, de l'incontestable mouvement qui, depuis plusieurs années, se produit en faveur des questions d'art. L'expansion artistique tend à tenir sa place dans la vie des nations.

Au milieu des vives controverses qu'a fait surgir parmi nous dans ces derniers temps la question de l'enseignement artistique, & qui n'ont, il faut l'avouer, abouti jusqu'à ce jour qu'à de mesquines personnalités, on a regretté de voir cette question rapetissée aux maigres proportions d'une rivalité de partis au lieu de se poser sur son véritable terrain, celui de l'*Art national*. Le goût public, épuré par l'étude des arts du passé, dont les spécimens remarquables viennent chaque jour grossir le trésor de nos musées & des collections particulières, semble de tous côtés diriger les efforts des artistes, non plus uniquement vers la création des types du beau absolu, mais encore & surtout vers les manifestations les plus *pratiques* de l'art : vers la décoration monumentale, vers l'ornementation du foyer domestique, vers l'embellissement de cette multitude d'objets nécessaires au bien-être intérieur.

La voie caractéristique dans laquelle notre art contemporain est appelé à se mouvoir désormais est ainsi bien nettement tracée : &, si les arts sont l'expression vivante & sensible d'une époque, ne serait-il pas désirable de voir diriger dans ce sens les études & les travaux de nos jeunes artistes, d'une vaillante génération d'artisans?

Loin de nous de songer à investir l'enseignement officiel de cette tâche : elle incombe, comme au temps passé[1], à l'initiative privée, & déjà nous voyons de louables efforts[2] se produire vers ce but. Mais, il faut bien le dire, en France, moins que partout ailleurs, rien n'est encore disposé pour la réorganisation du travail artistique, pour le développement de la production nationale d'art.

La grande tradition décorative, unique lien, seule & véritable base de la production artistique nationale, succomba chez nous, entraînée par l'abolition des priviléges, que décréta la République de 89. Religieusement transmise de génération en génération par la séculaire institution des corporations, jurandes & maîtrises, cette précieuse tradition se vit brusquement rompue par la subite explosion des idées libérales. Ses adeptes, tout un peuple d'artisans ingénieux et habiles, disséminés dans les quatorze

1. Nous voulons parler de l'institution des corporations.
2. La Société du Progrès de l'art industriel, fondée en 1858; la Société de l'Union centrale des beaux-Arts appliquées à l'industrie, fondée en 1863; les Concours régionaux, les Expositions des Sociétés libres des grands centres départementaux, etc.

PLATE 160. Title used for an editorial introduction. *L'Art pour tous*, 1864.

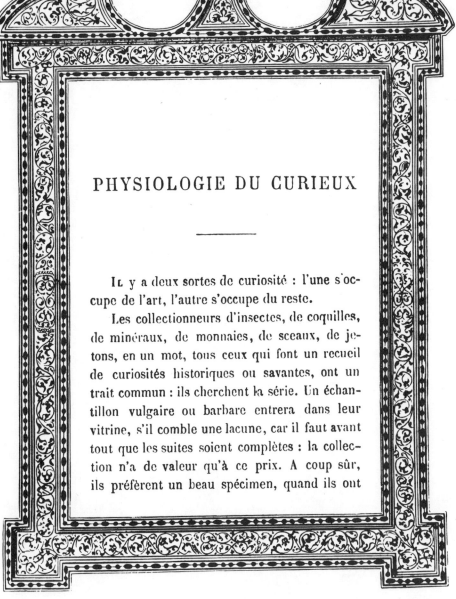

PHYSIOLOGIE DU CURIEUX

Il y a deux sortes de curiosité : l'une s'occupe de l'art, l'autre s'occupe du reste.

Les collectionneurs d'insectes, de coquilles, de minéraux, de monnaies, de sceaux, de jetons, en un mot, tous ceux qui font un recueil de curiosités historiques ou savantes, ont un trait commun : ils cherchent la série. Un échantillon vulgaire ou barbare entrera dans leur vitrine, s'il comble une lacune, car il faut avant tout que les suites soient complètes : la collection n'a de valeur qu'à ce prix. A coup sûr, ils préfèrent un beau spécimen, quand ils ont

PLATE 161. Title page of an article in the *Gazette des beaux arts*. 1880.

PLATE 162. Title for a music-college publication. Utrecht, 1881.

CLUB

LEYER und SCHWERT

ernennt hiemit

Herrn

zu seinem

Mitglied.

Vorstand: Secretär:

München,
den
18

PLATE 163. Membership certificate in the style of an 1880's title.

NAVIGATIO

PLATE 164. An Otto Hupp design, heavily influenced by Renaissance
ornament. 1884.

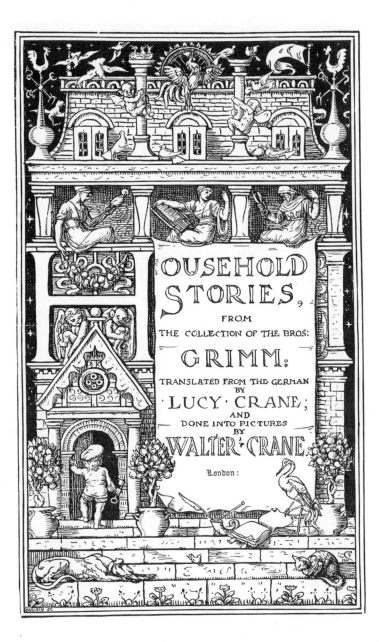

PLATE 165. A quite unusual title-page by Walter Crane. London, 1886.

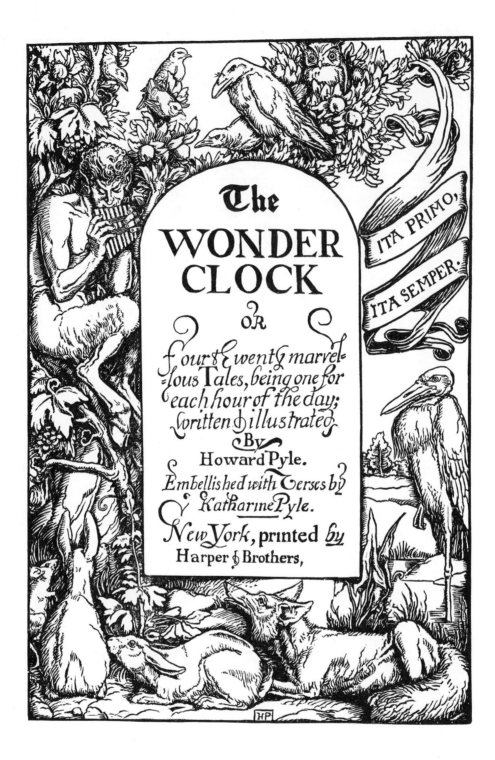

The
WONDER
CLOCK
OR
Four & Twenty marvellous Tales, being one for each hour of the day; written & illustrated By Howard Pyle. Embellished with Verses by Katharine Pyle. New York, printed by Harper & Brothers,

ITA PRIMO, ITA SEMPER.

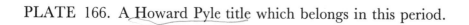

PLATE 166. A Howard Pyle title which belongs in this period.

PLATE 167. A curiously complicated title by Carloz Schwabe.   1892.

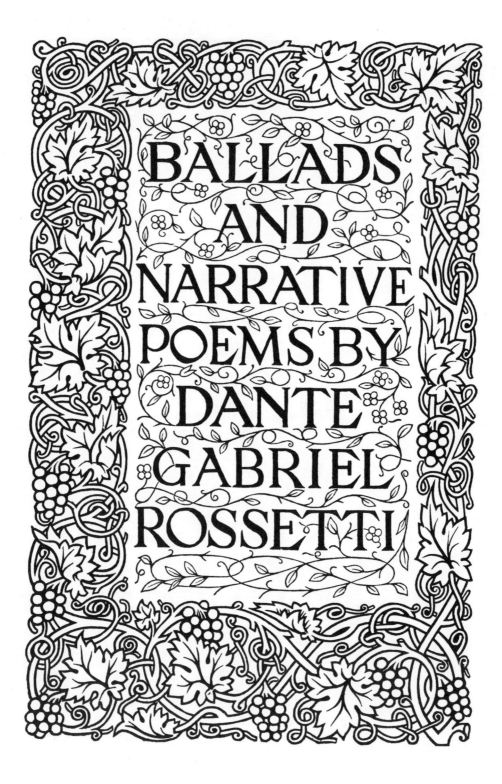

PLATE 168. The clarity and order of William Morris.   1893.

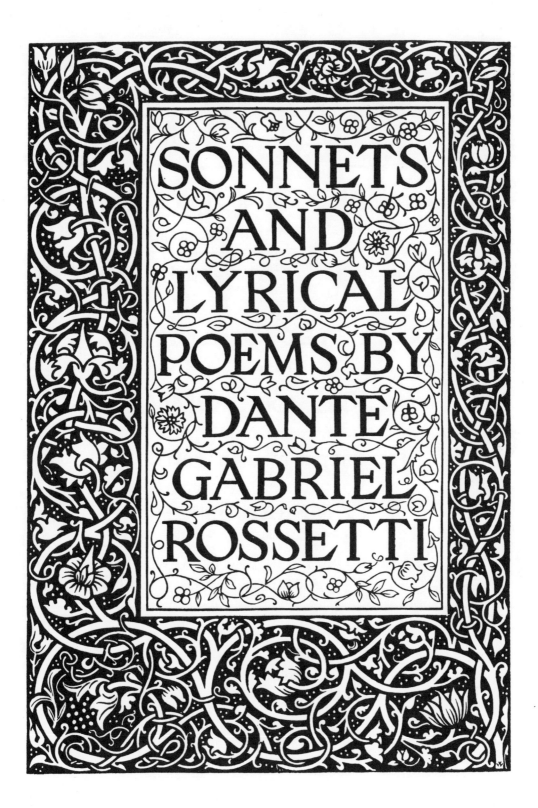

PLATE 169. A more typical Morris design, still of great vitality and interest. 1894.

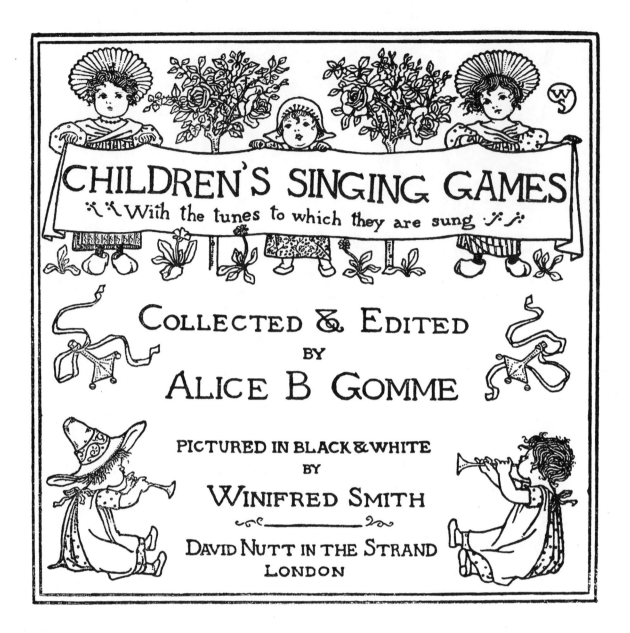

CHILDREN'S SINGING GAMES

With the tunes to which they are sung

COLLECTED & EDITED
BY
ALICE B GOMME

PICTURED IN BLACK & WHITE
BY
WINIFRED SMITH

DAVID NUTT IN THE STRAND
LONDON

PLATE 170. Title for a book of children's singing games.   London, 1894.

THE HOUSE
OF JOY

By LAURENCE
HOUSMAN

1895

LONDON: KEGAN PAUL
TRENCH TRUBNER & CO

PLATE 171. A title by Laurence Housman.   London, 1895.

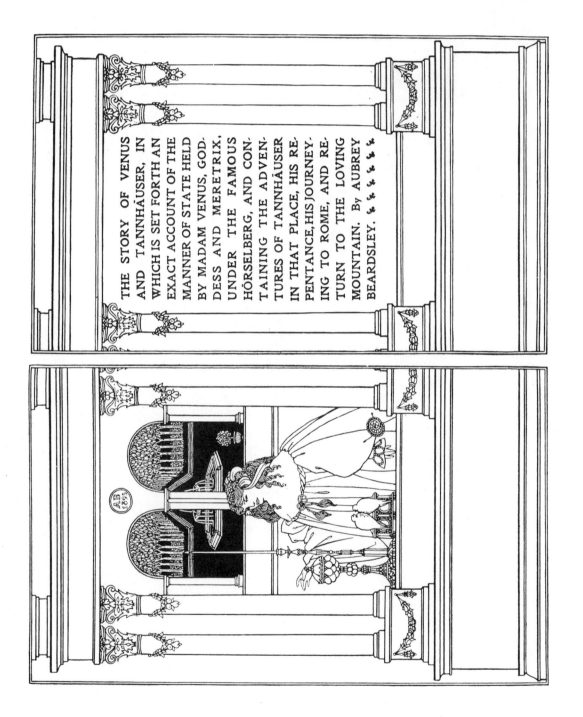

THE STORY OF VENUS AND TANNHÄUSER, IN WHICH IS SET FORTH AN EXACT ACCOUNT OF THE MANNER OF STATE HELD BY MADAM VENUS, GODDESS AND MERETRIX, UNDER THE FAMOUS HÖRSELBERG, AND CONTAINING THE ADVENTURES OF TANNHÄUSER IN THAT PLACE, HIS REPENTANCE, HIS JOURNEYING TO ROME, AND RETURN TO THE LOVING MOUNTAIN. By AUBREY BEARDSLEY.

PLATE 172. Combined frontispiece and title by Aubrey Beardsley. 1895.

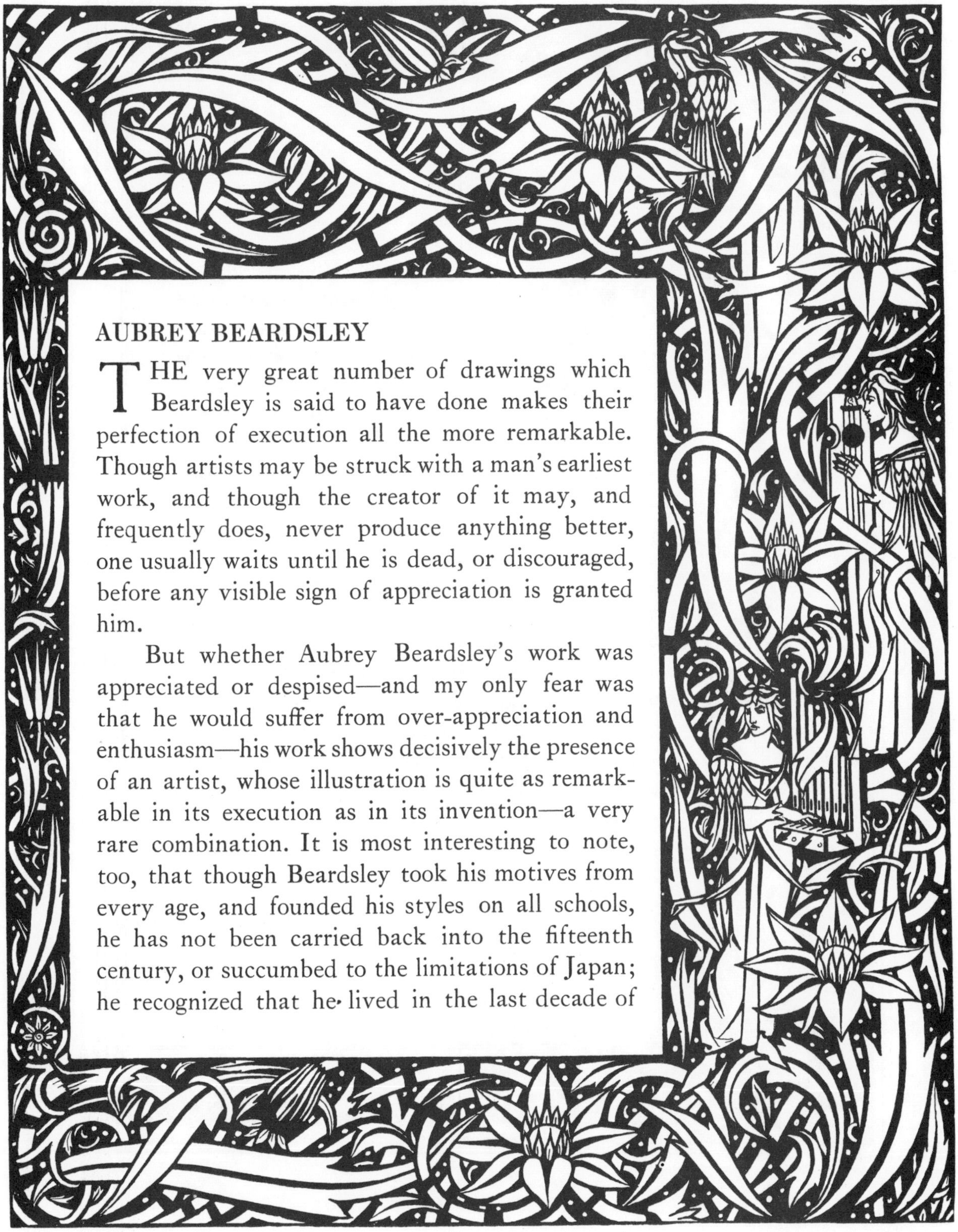

AUBREY BEARDSLEY

THE very great number of drawings which Beardsley is said to have done makes their perfection of execution all the more remarkable. Though artists may be struck with a man's earliest work, and though the creator of it may, and frequently does, never produce anything better, one usually waits until he is dead, or discouraged, before any visible sign of appreciation is granted him.

But whether Aubrey Beardsley's work was appreciated or despised—and my only fear was that he would suffer from over-appreciation and enthusiasm—his work shows decisively the presence of an artist, whose illustration is quite as remarkable in its execution as in its invention—a very rare combination. It is most interesting to note, too, that though Beardsley took his motives from every age, and founded his styles on all schools, he has not been carried back into the fifteenth century, or succumbed to the limitations of Japan; he recognized that he· lived in the last decade of

PLATE 173. The influence of Morris is evident in this Beardsley title.

Capriccío.

 etzte Tageshelle schmückt den Himmel, jene vorwurflose, leichte Klarheit, wie ich sie auf Ruisdaels Bildern so oft bewundere; wenige schwachdunkle Wolken hier und da. Venus freut sich schon ihres milden Glanzes; schräg unter ihr Jupiter; sonst ist kein Stern irgend zu entdecken. Jupiter ist doch bedeutend kleiner. So nahe bei seiner gefährlichen Nebenbuhlerin um die Herrschaft der Welt! Ob die beiden sich wohl hassen?

Auf einmal, was fällt euch denn nu ein? wirbeln sie um= einander, wie zwei Schmetterlinge, rechtsherum, linksherum, jetzt sich senkend, jetzt um so höher hinauf sich schwingend, um= gaukeln und übertollen sich, — sieh den Mond, wie er lacht, der alte dünne Gesell! — allein sie kümmern sich um nichts, kreuz und quer durch den ganzen Himmel geht das lustige Gejachter, über Süden und Norden und durch den Zenith, meine Augen sind längst müde zu folgen, der Nacken thut mir schon weh, — es giebt kein Aufhören; und ein himmlischer Rosenduft stäubt kühl von ihren goldenen Flügeln auf die Erde herunter.

Ausgetobt?

Da stehn sie wieder, als wäre nichts geschehen, rechts oben sie, links unten er, aber sie glänzen und strahlen noch schöner als vorhin.

Und um sie prangt das Heer unzähliger Gestirne.

Gustav Kühl.

PLATE 174. The great surge of *Jugendstil*. An Otto Eckmann design from *Pan*. 1895.

THE BARON SPIDERLEGS COVETS THE
BROAD ESTATES OF THE DRAGONFLIES.

PLATE 175. A Will Bradley border—the influence of Morris in the United
States.   1896.

LOVE'S SUICIDE.

Jean Wright.

Sweet Love lies dead,
    So stark and cold;
His golden head
    Rests on the mould.
Blood red roses
    flung at his feet,
Ah Love, fair Love,
    Thou wert so sweet!

So cold and stark
    Sweet Love lies slain;
Over his heart
    One crimson stain,
The fair dead past
    Can ne'er awake,
Love slew himself
    for his own dear sake.

PLATE 176. A border from Will Bradley's chapbook of December, 1896.

HERO AND LEANDER ↠ BY
CHRISTOPHER MARLOWE
AND
GEORGE CHAPMAN

Hero's description and her love's;
The fane of Venus where he moves
His worthy love-suit, and attains;
Whose bliss the wrath of Fates restrains
For Cupid's grace to Mercury:
Which tale the author doth imply.

PLATE 177. This title was produced by Charles Ricketts at the Vale Press.

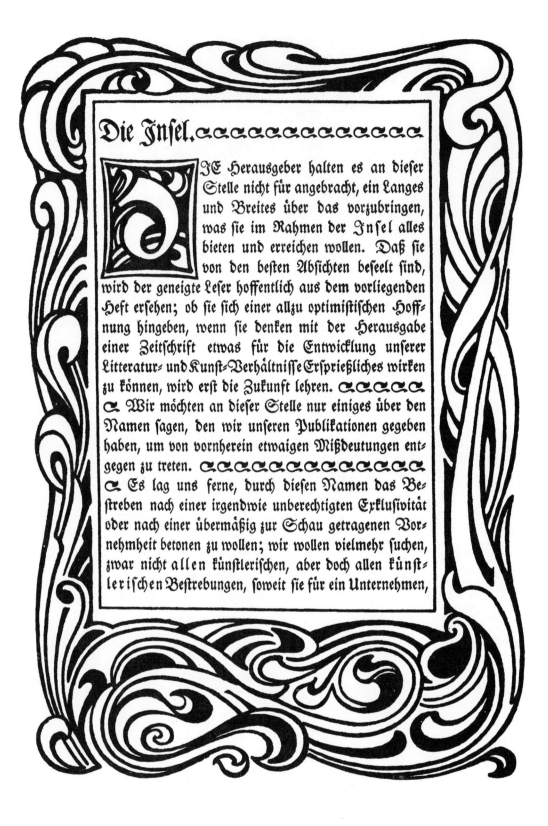

Die Insel. ᴄᴄᴄᴄᴄᴄᴄᴄᴄᴄᴄᴄ

IE Herausgeber halten es an dieſer Stelle nicht für angebracht, ein Langes und Breites über das vorzubringen, was ſie im Rahmen der Inſel alles bieten und erreichen wollen. Daß ſie von den beſten Abſichten beſeelt ſind, wird der geneigte Leſer hoffentlich aus dem vorliegenden Heft erſehen; ob ſie ſich einer allzu optimiſtiſchen Hoff= nung hingeben, wenn ſie denken mit der Herausgabe einer Zeitſchrift etwas für die Entwicklung unſerer Litteratur= und Kunſt=Verhältniſſe Erſprießliches wirken zu können, wird erſt die Zukunft lehren. ᴄᴄᴄᴄᴄ ᴄ Wir möchten an dieſer Stelle nur einiges über den Namen ſagen, den wir unſeren Publikationen gegeben haben, um von vornherein etwaigen Mißdeutungen ent= gegen zu treten. ᴄᴄᴄᴄᴄᴄᴄᴄᴄᴄᴄᴄ ᴄ Es lag uns ferne, durch dieſen Namen das Be= ſtreben nach einer irgendwie unberechtigten Exkluſivität oder nach einer übermäßig zur Schau getragenen Vor= nehmheit betonen zu wollen; wir wollen vielmehr ſuchen, zwar nicht allen künſtleriſchen, aber doch allen künſt= leriſchen Beſtrebungen, ſoweit ſie für ein Unternehmen,

PLATE 178. Again, the *Jugendstil* or *art nouveau*.   From *Die Insel*, 1899.

PLATE 179. A title by the American artist Arthur Parsons which fits into this period.

PLATE 180. A George Auriol design from *Art et décoration*, 1901.

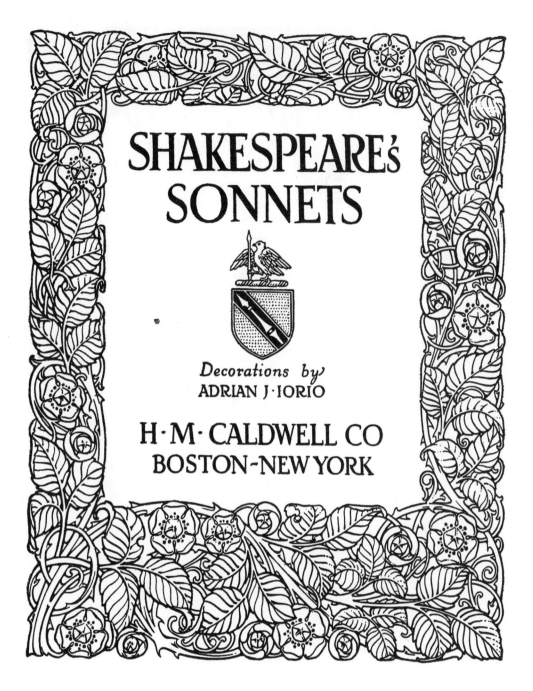

SHAKESPEARE's
SONNETS

Decorations by
ADRIAN J·IORIO

H·M·CALDWELL CO
BOSTON-NEW YORK

PLATE 181. The work of Adrian J. Iorio, a designer of the early 1900's.

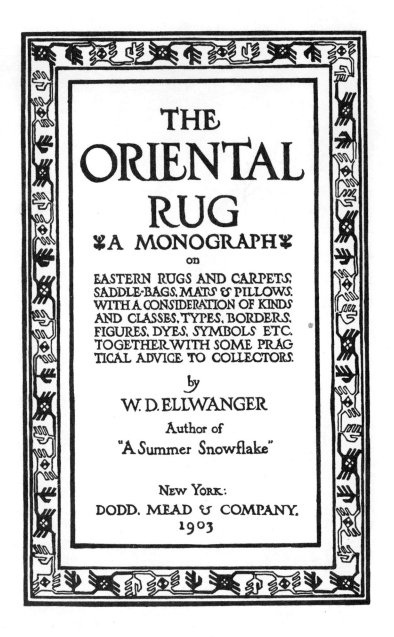

THE
ORIENTAL
RUG
❧ A MONOGRAPH ❧
on
EASTERN RUGS AND CARPETS,
SADDLE-BAGS, MATS & PILLOWS,
WITH A CONSIDERATION OF KINDS
AND CLASSES, TYPES, BORDERS,
FIGURES, DYES, SYMBOLS ETC.
TOGETHER WITH SOME PRAG
TICAL ADVICE TO COLLECTORS.

by

W. D. ELLWANGER

Author of
"A Summer Snowflake"

NEW YORK:
DODD, MEAD & COMPANY,
1903

PLATE 182. A title obviously based on a rug design. Typical 1903 lettering.

THE PRINCE OF
ILLUSION

JOHN LUTHER LONG

PLATE 183. *Jugendstil* in a more geometric arrangement. 1904.

PLATE 184. Titles by Bertram Grosvenor Goodhue and Theodore Brown
Hapgood, Jr. About 1904.

IV

By the way that Christ descended
  From Mount Olivet,
I, a lonely pilgrim, wended,
On the day his entry splendid
  Is remembered yet.

V

And I thought: If he, returning
  On this festival,
Here should haste with love and yearning,
Where would now his fearful, burning
  Anger flash and fall?

VI

In the very house they builded
  To his saving name,
'Mid their altars, gemmed and gilded,
Would his scourge and scorn be wielded,
  His fierce lightning flame.

VII

Once again, O Man of Wonder,
  Let thy voice be heard!
Speak as with a sound of thunder;
Drive the false thy roof from under;
  Teach thy priests thy word.

15

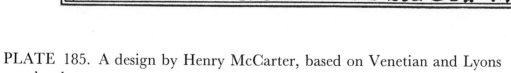

PLATE 185. A design by Henry McCarter, based on Venetian and Lyons borders. 1904.

·DEUTSCHE·KUNST· UND·DEKORATION·

·ZUM·3·JAHRGANG·

Der nunmehr abgeschlossene II. Jahrgang hat uns durch die ausserordentlich erweiterte Verbreitung unserer Zeitschrift den Beweis gebracht, dass der deutsche Geist in den modernen Gewerbe-Künsten siegreich voran drängt. Wir sind uns wohl bewusst, dass mit der erhöhten Entfaltung des künstlerischen Schaffens und mit dem sich fortwährend erweiternden Wirkungsgebiete unserer Hefte, auch an uns erhöhte Pflichten herantreten. Insbesondere erscheint es geboten, bei der Auswahl der zu veröffentlichenden Werke strengere Maassstäbe anzulegen, als dies wohl bisher mit Rücksicht auf die Unsicherheit, welche nun einmal in einer Zeit der Versuche und des Tastens Platz greifen muss, zu geschehen pflegte. Gar manche unserer Abbildungen der ersten Jahrgänge verdanken ja lediglich dieser Nachsicht ihre Aufnahme. Wir wurden dabei geleitet von der Ueberzeugung, dass es mitunter recht angebracht sei, zu zeigen, welche Gefahren auch dem Talente drohen in einer Epoche, in welcher die besonderen Voraussetzungen der angewandten Kunst noch nicht wieder in Fleisch und Blut übergegangen sind. Zudem darf nicht übersehen werden, dass auch an einer im Ganzen nicht entsprechenden Arbeit eines begabten Künstlers mitunter Einzelheiten Beachtung verdienen, sei es, dass sie die Begabung des Urhebers darthun und somit auf diesen aufmerksam machen, sei es, dass sie anderen, namentlich Männern der Praxis, Anregungen geben. Es wird wohl niemand im Ernste behaupten wollen, dass die Aufnahme einer Abbildung an sich schon bedeute, dass die Schriftleitung das betreffende Werk für einwandsfrei halte.

PLATE 186. A *Jugendstil* title from *Deutsche Kunst und Dekoration*. Paul Bürck, 1906.

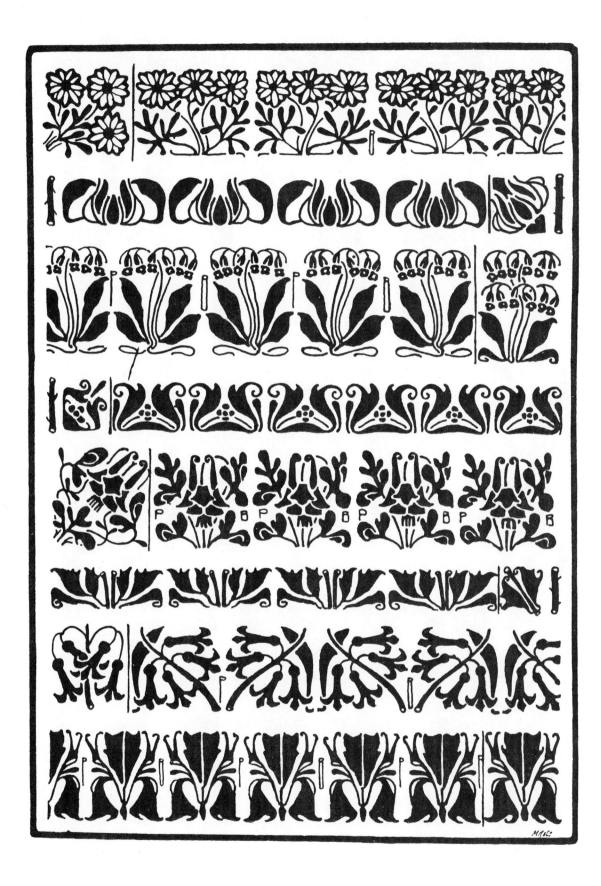

PLATE 187. Sketches for typographic border design motifs. Paul Bürck, 1906.

MOGANNI NAMEH · BUCH DES SÄN=
GERS

ZWANZIG JAHRE LIESS ICH GEHN
UND GENOSS, WAS MIR BESCHIEDEN;
EINE REIHE, VÖLLIG SCHÖN,
WIE DIE ZEIT DER BARMEKIDEN.

HEGIRE

ORD UND WEST UND
SÜD ZERSPLITTERN,
THRONE BERSTEN,
REICHE ZITTERN:
FLÜCHTE DU, IM REI=
NEN OSTEN,
PATRIARCHENLUFT
ZU KOSTEN!
UNTER LIEBEN, TRINKEN, SINGEN
SOLL DICH CHISERS QUELL VERJÜN=
GEN.

DORT, IM REINEN UND IM RECHTEN,
WILL ICH MENSCHLICHEN GE=
SCHLECHTEN
IN DES URSPRUNGS TIEFE DRINGEN,
WO SIE NOCH VON GOTT EMPFINGEN
HIMMELSLEHR IN ERDESPRACHEN
UND SICH NICHT DEN KOPF ZERBRA=
CHEN.

WO SIE VÄTER HOCH VEREHRTEN,
JEDEN FREMDEN DIENST VERWEHR-
TEN;
WILL MICH FREUN DER JUGEND=
SCHRANKE:

PLATE 188. From the Insel Verlag edition of Goethe's *Westöstlicher Divan.*   1910.

PLATE 189. A title-page produced in the Leipzig Akademie. 1910.

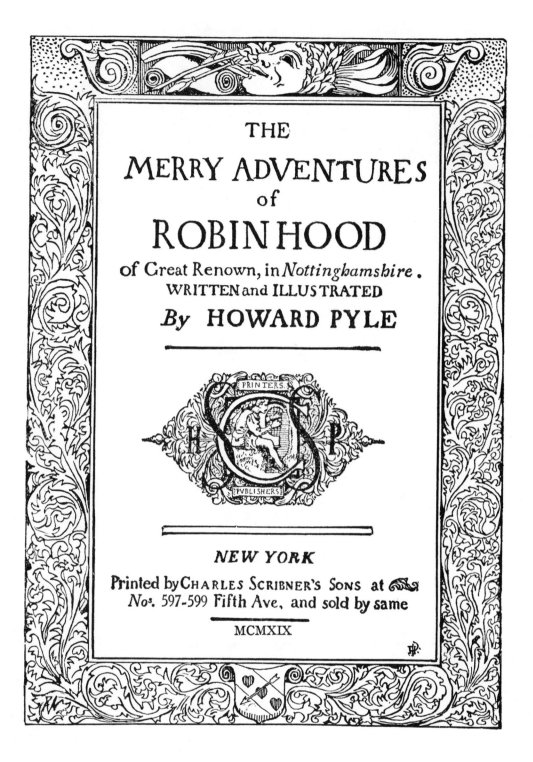

THE
MERRY ADVENTURES
of
ROBIN HOOD
of Great Renown, in *Nottinghamshire*.
WRITTEN and ILLUSTRATED
By HOWARD PYLE

PRINTERS.
H P
PVBLISHERS

NEW YORK
Printed by CHARLES SCRIBNER'S SONS at
Nos. 597-599 Fifth Ave, and sold by same
MCMXIX

PLATE 190. Another Howard Pyle title, 1919 edition.

PLATE 191. Insel Verlag edition of *1001 Nights*.   Title by Marcus Behmer.

Ce que doit être l'Etude de la NATURE Comment on doit l'INTERPRETER

□ □ □

J'AI déjà, dans un précédent numéro (janvier 1911), parlé de l'étude de la nature, et défini l'interprétation. Nous allons aujourd'hui étudier quelles sont les lois qui régissent celle-ci.

Il ne sera pas inutile, peut-être, de rappeler auparavant que l'interprétation est la transformation volontaire et réfléchie, sous des influences techniques et esthétiques, d'un élément nature pour l'amener à l'état ornemental. Nous avons établi aussi que le caractère de l'interprétation d'un motif nature est imposé en partie par la matière dans laquelle on le traduit, aussi bien que par les moyens de travail et d'expression que cette matière comporte. Nous savons donc parfaitement, maintenant, ce que l'on doit entendre par le mot interprétation.

Mais quelques généralités sont encore nécessaires avant d'étudier les lois qui président à l'interprétation. L'artiste peut, en effet, en interprétant une forme naturelle, se proposer des buts très différents. Il peut représenter cette forme dans ses caractères généraux ou dans ses caractères distinctifs et particuliers; ou pour parler plus clairement au moyen de quelques exemples: il peut se proposer de représenter un oiseau, dans son sens général d'être qui vole; ou un passereau, un échassier, ce qui précise davantage; ou un moineau, un héron, ce qui précise tout à fait. Donnons encore quelques exemples: il peut

PLATE 192. Title by M. P. Verneuil from *Art et décoration.* Original in two colors. 1912.

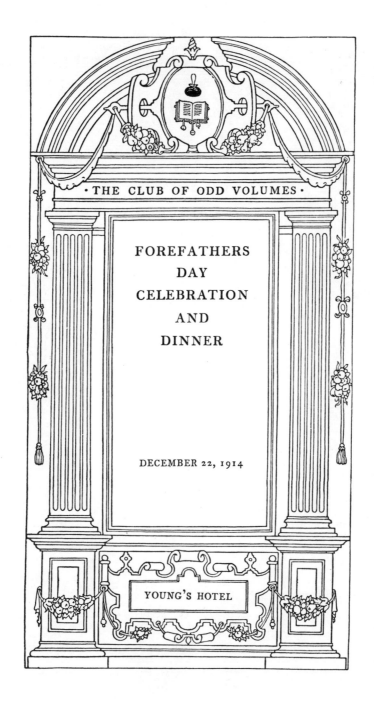

THE CLUB OF ODD VOLUMES

FOREFATHERS
DAY
CELEBRATION
AND
DINNER

DECEMBER 22, 1914

YOUNG'S HOTEL

PLATE 193. A Bruce Rogers title, typical of his period typography.

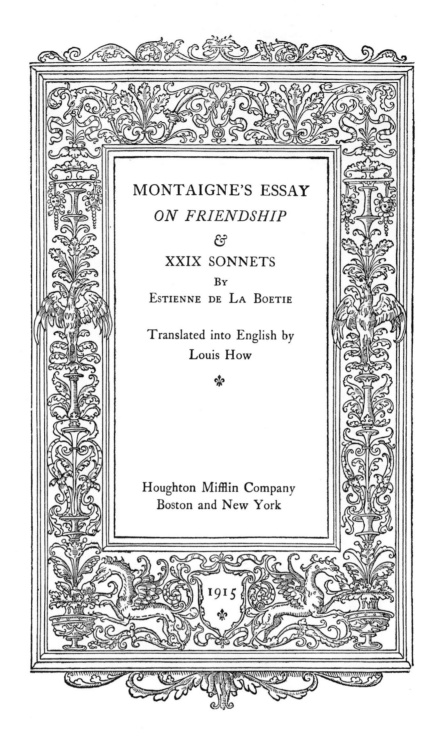

MONTAIGNE'S ESSAY

ON FRIENDSHIP

&

XXIX SONNETS

By

Estienne de La Boetie

Translated into English by
Louis How

❧

Houghton Mifflin Company
Boston and New York

1915

PLATE 194. The revival of earlier ornament; see plate 41.

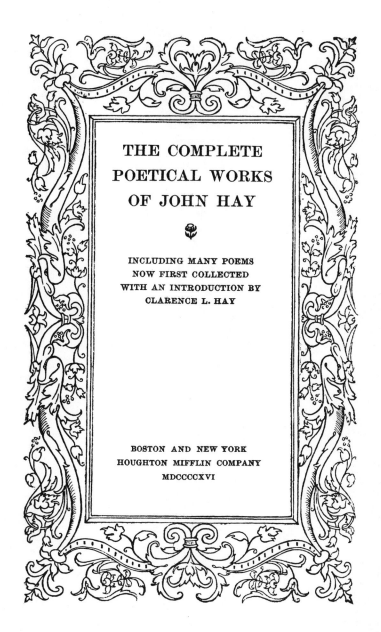

THE COMPLETE
POETICAL WORKS
OF JOHN HAY

INCLUDING MANY POEMS
NOW FIRST COLLECTED
WITH AN INTRODUCTION BY
CLARENCE L. HAY

BOSTON AND NEW YORK
HOUGHTON MIFFLIN COMPANY
MDCCCCXVI

PLATE 195. Another title based on sixteenth-century ornament. 1916.

FLOWERS
AND
FACES

BY

H. E. BATES

ENGRAVINGS

BY

JOHN NASH

**THE
GOLDEN COCKEREL
PRESS**

PLATE 196. The style of this title harks back to Callot.

PLATE 197. A title by the German type designer, Emil Rudolf Weiss.   1923.

Dichter

der Gegenwart

V

PAUL ZECH

Die junge Witwe

Sieben Gesänge

für eine dunkle

Frauenstimme

PLATE 198. This 1924 title is in the German geometric decorative style of the
1920's.

Mittwoch, den 12. März 1924

DON JUAN

Oper in zwei Aufzügen von Lorenzo da Ponte. Deutsch von Friedrich Rochlitz

Musik von Wolfgang Amadeus Mozart

★

Spielleitung: Willi Wirk

Musikalische Leitung: Bruno Walter

★

Personen

Don Juan	Josef Feinhals
Der Komtur	Paul Bender
Donna Anna, dessen Tochter	Nelly Merz
Don Octavio, deren Bräutigam . . .	Karl Erb
Donna Elvira, Don Juans verlassene Geliebte	Hermine Bosetti
Leporello, Don Juans Diener	Josef Geis
Masetto, ein Bauer	Alfred Bauberger
Zerline, dessen Braut	Maria Ivogün

Ein Arzt, Bauern und Bäuerinnen, Musikanten, Tänzer und Tänzerinnen, Diener

Ort: Sevilla. Zeit: Mitte des 17. Jahrhunderts

★

Anfang 7 Uhr / Nach dem 1. Aufzuge findet eine Pause statt / Ende 10 Uhr

PLATE 199. A title border by Anton Kling. 1924.

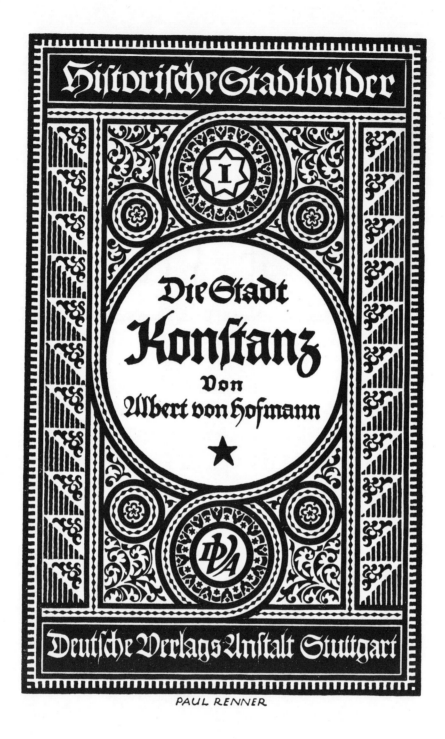

PLATE 200. A cover title drawn by the type designer Paul Renner, 1924.

Einfassungen

geben einem geschmackvollen Buchsatze
wie einem Anzeigentexte
den unbedingt notwendigen
wirkungsvollen
Rahmen

Seit 50 Jahren ist unsere Gießerei auf dem Gebiete der
Einfassungen führend tätig. Auch in den letzten Jahren
sind zahlreiche Neuheiten erschienen, mit denen den ver-
schiedensten Geschmacksrichtungen Rechnung getragen wird.
Die bekannte Sorgfalt unserer Gießtechnik verbürgt für
saubere Anschlüsse und den genauen Verlauf aller Linien
und Ansatzstücke

Eine reichhaltige Auswahl an Mustern
steht jederzeit zur Verfügung

J. G. Schelter & Giesecke
Leipzig C 1

PLATE 201. This title border was constructed typographically.   1926.

PLATE 202. A woodcut title by Fritz Richter.   1928.

EDLE

TYPOGRAPHISCHE SCHÖNHEIT

gibt den Erzeugnissen

des deutschen Buchdruckgewerbes

das Gepräge

In sinnfälligster Weise wird uns das an den Büchern klar, die aus den Offizinen der großen Druckstädte hervorgehen. Leipzig, Berlin, Stuttgart, München, um nur einige herauszugreifen, alle diese Orte haben im Druck und Verlag von Büchern nur mit Hilfe weitestgehender Verwendung maschineller Satzherstellungsmethoden Erfolge zeitigen können. Selbst kleine Werkdruckereien – von den namhaftesten ganz zu schweigen – haben die

MONOTYPE

in ihrer universellen Verwendbarkeit für einfachsten wie schwierigsten und kompliziertesten Satz längst erkannt und nutzbringend verwertet. Die Monotype steht als Einzelbuchstaben-Gieß-Setzmaschine einzig da. Absolut konkurrenzlos ist auch der Reichtum an schönen charaktervollen Fraktur- und Antiquaschriften, welcher der Monotype zur Verfügung steht. Das Ideal neuzeitlichen, buchgewerblichen Schaffens, mechanisch erzeugten Satz in der Güte tadellosem Handsatz ebenbürtig erscheinen zu lassen, hat einzig und allein die Monotype restlos verwirklicht. Ziehen Sie aus diesen anerkannten Tatsachen die Nutzanwendung: Ihr Betrieb darf nicht länger ohne die Monotype-Anlage arbeiten!

MONOTYPE

SETZMASCHINEN-VERTRIEBS-GESELLSCHAFT M. B. H.

BERLIN SW 61 / KREUZBERGSTR. 30

PLATE 203. A border made by using monotype flowers. 1929.

Bibliography and Sources of the Plates

The plates in the present work were compiled mostly from facsimiles appearing in the works which have been listed below for the reader who wishes to investigate further the history of the decorative title-page. Wherever appropriate, the bibliographical entry is followed by the numbers (in **bold-face** type) of the plates in the present work taken from it.

Certain of the plates were made directly from original title-pages or from facsimiles in sources not readily identifiable. A list of the numbers of these plates is given at the end of the Bibliography.

Das alte Buch, by Karl Schottenloher, published by Klinkhardt & Biermann, Braunschweig, 1956.

Das alte Buch und seine Ausstattung vom XV bis zum XIX Jahrhundert. Buchdruck, Buchschmuck und Einbände, a portfolio in the *Quelle* series, No. 13, foreword by Dr. Heinrich Röttinger, Vienna, 1915.

Archiv für Buchgewerbe und Gebrauchsgraphik, published by Verlag des deutschen Buchgewerbevereins zu Leipzig. Heft 1, 1924—Plates **191, 199, 200.** Heft 4, 1924—**198.** Heft 6, 1926—**201.** Heft 8, 1926—**142, 174, 178, 188.** Heft 10/12, 1927—**197.** Heft 8, 1929—**203.** Heft 9, 1929—**202.**

Archiv für Druck und Papier; internationale Fachzeitschrift, published by Buch- und Druckgewerbe Verlag K.G., Berlin, Heft 3, 1956—**138.**

Art et décoration, a magazine founded in 1897, Paris. 1901—**180.** 1912—**192.**

The Art of the Book, by Bernard Newdigate, published by The Studio, Ltd., London, and Studio Publications, New York, 1938.

L'art pour tous; encyclopédie de l'art industriel et décoratif, a magazine founded in 1860 by Émile Reiber, Paris. 1860—**73.** 1862—**102, 114, 115.** 1863—**82, 95, 129, 159 top.** 1864—**159 bottom, 160.** 1867—**125.** 1868—**124, 126.**

Aventur und Kunst; eine Chronik des Buchdruckgewerbes von der Erfindung der beweglichen Letter bis zur Gegenwart, compiled by Konrad F. Bauer, printed privately by the Bauer Type Foundry, Frankfurt am Main, 1940—**1.**

Beauties of the Opera and Ballet, under the superintendence of Mr. Charles Heath, published by David Bogue, London, probably 1844—**149, 150, 151, 152, 153, 154, 155.**

Die Bücherornamentik der Hoch- und Spätrenaissance, a portfolio in two parts of facsimiles compiled by Albert Fidelis Butsch, published by Georg Hirth, Leipzig, 1878 and 1881—**2, 4, 5, 6, 7, 9, 10, 12, 13, 14, 15, 16, 17, 18, 19, 20, 21, 22, 23, 24, 25, 26, 29, 30, 33, 36, 37, 40, 53, 54, 56, 57, 63, 67, 80.**

A Catalogue of Engraved and Etched English Title-Pages Down to the Death of William Faithorne, 1691, compiled by Alfred Forbes Johnson, printed for the Bibliographical Society at the Oxford University Press, London, 1934 for 1933—**74, 81, 86, 88, 103, 104, 107, 108, 109, 110.**

The Charles Whittinghams Printers, by Arthur Warren, published by The Grolier Club, New York, 1896.

Deutsche Kunst und Dekoration, a magazine founded in 1897. 1906—**186, 187.**

Der Formenschatz, a portfolio of facsimiles published by Georg Hirth, Leipzig, during the 1880's—**31, 34, 39, 43, 44, 45, 47, 50, 58, 59, 66, 77, 83, 99, 105, 111, 112, 113, 117, 119, 120, 121, 122, 123, 127, 128, 133, 135, 136.**

Four Centuries of Fine Printing, by Stanley Morison, published by Ernest Benn, Ltd., London, 1924. Revised edition published in smaller format by Farrar, Straus & Co., New York, 1949.

French Sixteenth Century Printing, by A. F. Johnson, published by Charles Scribner's Sons in the "Periods of Typography" series, New York, 1928.

Gazette des beaux arts; Courrier européen de l'art et de la curiosité, Paris, 1880—**161.**

Initialen, Alphabete und Randleisten verschiedener Kunstepochen, a portfolio of facsimiles compiled by Carl Hrachowina, published by Carl Graeser, Vienna, 1883 and 1897—**90, 116.**

The Italian Sixteenth Century, by A. F. Johnson, published by Ernest Benn, Ltd., in the "Periods of Typography" series, London, 1926.

Jugendstil, by Ewald Rathke, published by Bibliographisches Institut AG, Mannheim, 1958 (paperback).

Last Words on the History of the Title-Page with Notes on Some Colophons and Twenty-Seven Fac-similes of Title-Pages, by Alfred W. Pollard, published by John C. Nimmo, London, 1891.

The Later Work of Aubrey Beardsley, published by The Bodley Head, Ltd., London, 1900—**172.**

Of the Decorative Illustration of Books Old and New, by Walter Crane, published by George Bell and Sons, London, 1901—**171, 177.**

One Hundred Title Pages, 1500-1800, selected and arranged with an Introduction and notes by A. F. Johnson, published by John Lane, The Bodley Head, Ltd., London, 1928—**11, 32, 35, 38, 41, 42, 46, 48, 49, 51, 52, 55, 60, 70, 75, 76, 78, 130, 131, 132, 134.**

Pen Drawing and Pen Draughtsmen, by Joseph Pennell, published by I. Fisher Unwin Ltd., London, 1921—**167, 173, 179.**

The Printing Art, edited by Henry Lewis Johnson, published by the University Press, Cambridge, Massachusetts, 1903 and 1904—**181, 182, 183, 184, 185.**

Title-Page Borders Used in England and Scotland, 1485-1640, by R. B. McKerrow and E. S. Ferguson, printed for the Bibliographical Society at the Oxford University Press, London, 1932—**8, 61, 62, 64, 65, 79, 85, 87, 89, 91, 92, 93, 94, 96, 97, 98, 100, 101.**

Title Pages as Seen by a Printer, With Numerous Illustrations in Facsimile and Some Observations on the Early and Recent Printing of Books, by Theodore Low de Vinne, published by The Grolier Club, New York, 1901.

A Treatise on Title-Pages, by Theodore Low de Vinne, published by the Century Company in the "Practice of Typography" series, New York, 1902 (a popular edition of the preceding Grolier Club book, with additions in the practical area and a greater number of pages).

Um 1900; Art Nouveau und Jugendstil, Kunst und Kunstgewerbe aus Europa und Amerika zur Zeit der Stilwende, catalog of an exhibition at the Kunstgewerbemuseum, Zürich, 1952.

William Morris Designer, by Gerald H. Crow, special winter number of *The Studio*, published by The Studio, Ltd., London, 1934.

Plates from sources not readily identifiable—**3, 27, 28, 68, 69, 71, 72, 84, 106, 118, 137, 139, 140, 141, 143, 144, 145, 146, 147, 148, 156, 157, 158, 162, 163, 164, 165, 166, 168, 169, 170, 175, 176, 189, 190, 193, 194, 195, 196.**